Path of Fire and Light

VOLUME 2

Path of Fire and Light
Volume 2

Swami Rama

The Himalayan Institute Press
Honesdale, Pennsylvania

The Himalayan Institute Press
RR 1, Box 405
Honesdale, Pennsylvania 18431

Cover design by Robert Aulicino

The paper used in this publication meets the minimum
requirements of American National Standard for Information
Sciences—Permanence of Paper for Printed Library
Materials, ANSI Z39.48-1984.

The Library of Congress has catalogued Volume 1 as follows:

Rama, Swami, 1925 -
        Path of fire and light.

        Includes index.
        1. Breathing exercises. 2. Yoga, Hatha. I. Title.
RA782.R34 1986   613.7'046   86-7586
ISBN 0-89389-097-9

Volume 2 ISBN: 0-89389-112-6

Contents

Publisher's Note

The Himalayan Institute Press is honored to make available to readers Sri Swami Rama's book *Path of Fire and Light, Volume 2*. It is meant to be a practical companion text to volume 1 of *Path of Fire and Light*, and to complement and clarify that material. It also stands on its own as a profound work on philosophy and practice.

The text of this book has been edited from an advanced seminar taught by Sri Swami Rama at the Himalayan Institute in the summer of 1987, and we have tried to preserve the natural quality of Swamiji's spoken words. This material forms a beautiful and sound philosophical framework for the practice of yoga at all levels, and also offers a number of specific practices for experienced students.

It is never recommended that students attempt to learn practices in yoga from books alone, as they may experience adverse effects if they are not sufficiently prepared. Personal instruction in this tradition of meditation is available at the Himalayan Institute headquarters and its branch centers and affiliated centers around the world.

The Lord of Life in the Universe is within me.

I am not the body, but a shrine of that Lord,
the Lord of Love and Life.

Through my thoughts, speech, and actions
I will emanate love.

CHAPTER ONE

The Philosophy of Life

THE SUN, THE MOON, THE STARS, and all the lights that you can imagine in the entire external world are but fragments of that one great Light that is within you. It is the light of knowledge, the light of discrimination, the light of understanding, the light of life, the light of sharing and love, the light of Being that you are. "Thou art that."

The light within is like a ripple in the vast ocean of bliss—that which we call Brahman, the Absolute, Infinity, the Highest. You yourself are that ripple; you are a wave. You should always have confidence that the light of life really is within you. Physics corroborates this philosophy; it also says that life is like a particle, like a wave. It repeats the ancient philosophy that tells us that life is a wave born from the ocean of bliss, playing in it, and subsiding again into it.

There is nothing that is truly subject to death. The Vedas, the most ancient scriptures in the library of humanity, say that after this universe goes into annihilation, it returns again. The sun, moon, and stars shine again in the same way that they did before. Essentially nothing dies; we also do not die. How can we die? To think that we die is a weak philosophy. If God is everywhere, what dies? Where is that which dies? The idea that one is completely annihilated is philosophically inaccurate.

You need to understand something about life and the universe first before we discuss practical spiritual techniques, because no technique is complete if you do not have an individual philosophy. If you do not understand these things before undertaking spiritual practices, these questions will preoccupy your mind, disturbing your practice. Thus, your individual philosophy should be well understood. You are all philosophers; you lack only a specific philosophy, because your thinking is undisciplined and your mind is undirected. No complete technique is taught to help you experience the light no matter where you go. There is no tradition, country, or culture where the mind is taught to see, watch, will, and find what it seeks. Books inform you about that philosophy, teachers share their experiences and knowledge, but you must also have the capacity to use that knowledge.

In some ways Westerners, especially the American people, are very fortunate. There is something great in you. You do not know your history or see how you move, but you move with confidence. Your country is large, you are secure, and it is easy for you to earn a living. You are also personally secure. So if you are really searching for something, you can attain it. However, because of the influence of your popular culture you think only in a material way; you cannot think of or understand the goal and aim of life. You cry for that sense of purpose. That is why some of you take drugs, thinking that drugs are higher than Christ. You do not receive training in the goals of life because there is no culture that teaches and understands the aim of life. True culture really belongs to the great sages. Spiritual culture has been flowing since eternity, and we all have a right to it. Life is a line, hung on two points. One point is called birth and the other is called death. We see and understand life through the windows of our vision. We now have limited vision because we see a limited horizon. We see that we are born and that we die, yet we do not know either how we are born or how we die. Who is really responsible for your birth in this world? Parents? Your parents are the means of your birth, but if you are only a result of their choice, then why do you not have exactly their character and all their qualities? Why do you grow to be a separate individual in a different way from them? These are questions you should understand: from where have you come? who brought you to this earth? and where will you go?

In searching for comfort people say, "God brought me to this world," but that is not a full explanation. Religionists push such questions aside and enter the path of devotion. To lead people on the path of faith and devotion is good; it helps people and gives them solace. But it is better for you to understand that by dismissing questions the mind can create serious problems for you. Your faith is challenged by your own mind and reason.

I am not criticizing faith. Faith is very good, provided that it is reasoned faith. The particular capacity of the mind that reasons should go hand in hand with faith. If it does not, eventually—after a few days, a few months, or a few years—you will find that although you walked very well, with all your strength, you were walking backwards, and you will find yourself a thousand miles further away from your goal.

You are like a manuscript, not a completed book. A book has a beginning, a middle, and an end. It is printed by machines in a press and bound as a permanent unit. But you do not know from where you have come or where you will go. You are in search of the beginning and ending pages of life in order to make your manuscript complete. My purpose now is to help you understand how to search for the missing pages of life's manuscript.

Your desires bring you into this world. In the same way that an accountant uses a new ledger book while the accounts remain the same, so we bring forward all of our past accounts and simply copy them into new books. Your body is new, your brain is new, your conscious mind is new, but the desires that motivate you to come to this world are old. Desire with a certain motivation causes rebirth. Birth is our coming forward from the unknown and the unseen, from the hidden part of life. In Sanskrit, there are three words used for this concept: *srishti, janman,* and *utpatti.* These three words mean, respectively, "that which is hidden and comes forward," "that which was behind comes forward," and "that which was unknown and unseen comes forward." You do not die. You are immortal beings.

The wheel of the universe rotates continuously, nonstop; its nature is to rotate. In that rotation a time comes when we become human beings. Humans are the most advanced of all species—those who can both think and narrate. When the wheel rotates and you gain human status, then you become responsible. With the status of a thinking, narrating being, you take on responsibility. The activities of human beings are not controlled by nature. Human beings can always attain victory over nature. The room you are in now is a victory over nature;

it protects you from cold and heat and from other external disturbances. So you are not simply an animal; you are a sophisticated animal with understanding and knowledge. And if the Almighty, as you may call it, is ultimately responsible for all this, then why are you worried? As God has made you, with understanding and knowledge, so you are. You are responsible for your actions, and once your state in life has been given to you, you are also responsible for what you do in the world.

You are the master of your destiny; no one else created that destiny for you. You are the master of your destiny both consciously and sometimes also unconsciously. At present you have no control over your unconscious mind, that part of the mind that is unknown to you, yet it motivates you to do certain things. By analyzing your actions, you can learn about your unconscious mind. It is only an aspect of mind that stands as a wall between you and the Reality, between the gross and the subtle aspects of yourself.

If you have no knowledge about yourself, what can you understand about the universe? How can you understand your relationship with the universe? If you do not understand these matters, then remembering God's name, praying, or meditating is merely escapism or helplessness, because you have no direction. You have accepted what you were taught: that you cannot understand and that you are helpless. You need to explore and understand how you came to this world, why you came, what death is, and how you go again into that whirlpool of life.

No one can give you anything; you have to light your own lamp. Nobody gives you salvation. Do not become dependent upon any external resource, for no one has the power to give you salvation if you do not want it and will not work for it. You should have a burning desire for salvation. You should have a wick, oil, and a lamp to light the flame, and then there will be light. But if you do not have all these at one time, then creating light is not possible. The question is how to put them together. You should learn techniques and practice, and you should also know the philosophy of life.

You are responsible for your actions, whatever you have done. You have the power to do certain actions, and when you reap the fruits of those actions, then they motivate you to do still more actions. In this manner you have become a great collector of duties and responsibilities. Because of this, no one can help you; you have to help yourself.

So our work is to analyze this incomplete manuscript of life and to explore what happened to the manuscript here and there. It is not necessary for you to understand everything about your past. You should not torment yourself in trying to learn it. If you do not understand your past, you are not ignorant, you are merely innocent. You are here at a certain point in this present life. By understanding your present situation you can understand the future and the past. The manuscript of your life has been written by you.

Whether you hate or love yourself, you have to put up with and eventually accept yourself. If you accept yourself and your duties willingly, it is good. If you do not, but instead resist your duties, you will be miserable. One who is truly learned understands this. Even a doctor of philosophy or psychology is not truly learned, because he has only read a few books—he does not know anything profound about why he came to this plane and where he will go. One who is truly learned has that knowledge.

Your responsibility does not lie in other kingdoms—in the kingdoms of animals, vegetables, or rocks—it lies only in the kingdom of human beings. You have your own will. You are the creator of your own destiny. You are the master of all you survey. That is the difference between you and the other species or kingdoms of the world. That is why this law is accepted universally: "As you sow, so shall you reap."

My master used to teach about a book called *Khandakam*. He taught my brother disciple, my *gurubhai*, while I sat next to him. Thirteen times my master taught him the same lesson, but whenever my gurubhai was asked a question, he could not answer. One day my master threw his wooden sandal at my gurubhai's head and said, "You sandal-head! Don't you understand? I've been teaching you and teaching you, but where is your mind?" Then he threw another sandal and hit me. I still carry the scar on my forehead to remind me.

Why did that happen to me? Because of the law of association. Sometimes you suffer misfortune not because of your own deeds but because you are associated with somebody else. You suffer because of that person. You need to understand this law of karma, to understand how the law of karma becomes active, how you are caught in its whirlpool, and why it is so important.

So given this law, how can you gain freedom from your own actions? Philosophically it can be explained, but understanding this philosophy will not free you until you practice it. If you work selflessly for me and I work selflessly for you, then we will both be free. Actually, all coupling—the process of creating relationships in the world—is meant to help us attain that freedom. If a wife loves her husband and works for him, and the husband loves his wife and works for her, then there is a mutual understanding. Both will be free of the consequences of their actions. But that does not usually happen. Both partners usually expect too much and make their home miserable, instead of radiating their love toward the other. If you consider your own body, you know that your feet and hands work together. All your parts and organs work for the good of the whole, and because each part is working for the others, your body becomes a whole living machine. But we do not live that way in the external world, and that is why we suffer.

The flow of communication is broken because you do not perceive your common identity with others. When you do not understand your common purpose or identity with others, you expect others to give you love, to share love with you, and to help you. That cannot happen unless you understand yourself first. Suffering will no longer exist in the world and the flower of humanity will bloom on the day that we understand that to remain free we will have to work for the good of each other. Freedom alone is a prominent desire of all human beings, and external love is one step toward freedom.

The most important thing is that we are human beings, and being human, we should attain the next step. That next step is fulfillment, unfoldment, perfection, and enlightenment. Do you know what this word "enlightenment" means? It does not mean to become inhuman or perfect. To be perfect would be perfectly boring! To be enlightened does not mean one does not do normal things, like talking or eating. Do not do others the injustice of expecting people to become inhuman.

In this book I will tell you what I know, based on my experiences. I will share with you the knowledge of what

I have practiced, which I received through my studies and experiences with the sages. No matter what religion you follow or believe, if you follow these practices methodically you will definitely gain progress.

What does it mean to practice? Start practicing what you have known. The modern world is oriented to the concept of time. So we always ask, "How long will the process take?" I can teach it systematically, but what is your capacity for practice? If I know that, then I can tell you how long it will take. You must know your own capacity. Are you really a fully determined person? Are you determined that you want to know yourself? Or do you want to dismiss this goal? The human mind is very small; it is like a small ruler or scale. And with the help of that small scale alone you cannot measure this vast universe and that eternity and infinity.

You can use your mind up to a certain point, but beyond that, you cannot benefit from using your mind. You can learn how to use your mind in a creative way, and you can learn at what point the mind should be surrendered. If the mind is not finally surrendered, then the flow of intuitive knowledge, that internal library of infinite knowledge, will not flow. Without it, you remain only on the surface of your conscious mind.

So you have to do two things: you must learn how to make the best use of your mind, and then how to go beyond the realm of the mind. Avoiding the use of your mind will not help you. Reading and studying are good pastimes, but reading does not lead you very far. You only gather information. The important thing is to practice, practice, practice! By practicing, even the worst student receives something and experiences something.

Not all experiences guide us, however. Only rare

experiences—those that come from beyond, from the inner dimension, rather than from bodily sensations, the mind, or the senses—can really guide us. These experiences come when you are not moving. They cannot come when you are moving, because then your mind is busy. Physicists say that everything is subject to movement in the external world; all the particles of everything are moving. The mind is also moving. The human mind is like a drunken monkey; it wants to jump from one place to another, seeking externally the solace and peace that are already within.

Many of you think that your mind can be controlled. That is not a useful idea. Like the monkey, the mind can never actually be controlled; it can only be directed. If you want to try to control your mind, you will regret the results. Forget the word "control" and learn to direct your mind and energy on all levels. The moving mind wants to know things, to collect data from the things that are moving outside. To do that, you have to learn to be still. That stillness should not be forced; it should come through wisdom, and it should be easy.

The systems of prayer, meditation, and contemplation all agree on the need for stillness. These approaches are not separate; they help each other. So do not misunderstand and think that meditators condemn prayer or suggest that you should not pray. But most of the time those who pray are asking, "Give me this, give me this, give me this." They do not understand that when you pray, you are actually praying to your higher self.

Meditation is also sometimes misused by those who cannot handle things and want to escape. This is not the purpose of meditation. Contemplation is the school that teaches you how to think about the higher issues of life.

It teaches the meaning of truth. Suppose I am a truthful person and I meet someone who appears very happy but who lies constantly. Do I become sad and unhappy while practicing truthfulness? Such questions can be resolved through contemplation. The first thing you should know is that you have come to this earth as a human being, and a human being has the power to perform actions. So understand the purpose of human action—the philosophy of selfless actions. This is the philosophy of self-surrender.

What does it mean to surrender? Humans cannot avoid acting in the world, and whenever you act, you reap the fruits of those actions. When you reap those fruits then the fruits themselves motivate you to do more action, and then there is the whirlpool for you. So the best goal is to learn to share the fruits of your action. Your immediate field of practice in sharing should be your family. This happens very naturally with a mother and child. The mother shares and gives, but the child does not yet share. The mother gives birth to the child, she cares for it, she does so much for it, but if she wants something so small as a candy from the child's hand, the child will not share it.

Why do you create barriers and obstacles in your life, between yourself and your friends, spouse, and parents? Because you are selfish and do not want to share. You have to learn to share, for sharing alone liberates us. You create a wall around yourself; you create a fortress that is not helpful. You create all these blocks between yourself and others and then go from this person to that one. You have to learn to help yourself, to remove these blocks independently. This is called self-therapy. Then you know how far you have gone and how far you still have to go.

When one speaks about spiritual paths, the element of fire is often mentioned. So let us explain what that fire is. Fire helps you to live. Fire gives warmth; it is the warmth of life. If you lose the warmth of your body, there is no charm in life, and you will die. But where does fire dwell in the body? How do you get that fire of life? Where does it originate and how can you lead and channel it? What happens when you begin to work with it? Is that fire self-existent, or is it dependent on something else?

The ascending power of fire within you is the fire of love, the sharing of love with others in relationships, the love and caring for your family and your friends, and the love of your duties, without which you cannot survive. It requires the help of a descending power. That descending power is what you call grace.

You should understand the difference between the ascending and descending powers, and how they work in your body. Your human effort learns to work with the ascending power, but human effort alone cannot cause the dawning of wisdom. There is an ancient saying: "When the disciple is ready, the guru appears." *Guru* means "wisdom." As there is only one life-force, so there is only one wisdom, only one fountain of knowledge, life, and light. How does this power of wisdom descend, and from where does it come?

To know this, you have to understand both parts of the process: the fire that ascends, and the light that dawns. Grace comes to a human being when he or she has completed their own work. No one receives grace without first doing work themselves; otherwise, the law of cause and effect would be disturbed. That law says that you have to make your own endeavor. It does not matter if you fail. The important thing is your real effort. After that, grace and wisdom appear.

If you want to know what grace actually is, there are four aspects to it: the grace of God, the grace of the Bible or scriptures, the grace of the guru, and—most importantly—the grace of the self. If there is no grace of the self, then nothing is going to happen: all these other graces do not work. But if you have the grace of the self, then these other graces work.

If you are satisfied with all the little toys, pleasures, and sweets you are getting in the world, then you will not gain the more important goal. But if you do not settle for life's small pleasures, then the ultimate goal will be yours. Everyone feels a lack of satisfaction with life and its pleasures, but sometimes we push it aside to follow the path of escapism. Sometimes we become very pessimistic, negative, or depressed. It is necessary to develop and strengthen the flame of desire for higher goals. You have to practice nurturing it. At first it is a small flame of light and life. But by feeding it and allowing it to grow, it will become like a raging forest fire. Then the flame of desire for the Ultimate cannot be put out by any means.

Initially the disturbances of the external world and its charms and temptations will disturb you and create problems for you. That is because your desire is a tiny flame. But when you have protected it and allowed the flame to grow, then no one can stop it. Then you do not need to protect it, because it, itself, burns up all that disturbs you. That fire and light is really within you. That is why the great Upanishads say, "Thou art that": thou art the Absolute.

Sometimes you want to accomplish something, but you do not have the determination, the clarity, the wisdom, or the fearlessness. Because you lack these skills you repeatedly experience setbacks in life. You have many fears in your mind and heart that hold you back. All your life you labor under the pressure of these fears. They remain because you have never examined them. You keep them in your heart and mind and do not share them, even with the best and closest of your friends. Your ego does not allow you to talk about them even to your teachers, your spouse, or someone whom you love, because you think that your personality will be misunderstood, or that you might lose something if you discuss your fears. Every human being is afraid in this same way; every human being is inhibited by fears. But all your fears should be examined, so that you can remain fearless as long as you live. If you want to live, why not live fearlessly? There is no charm in a life full of fear. You should not accept this fearful sort of living. Fearless living is possible when you have understood the way to do your actions in the external world and when you have learned about your internal states.

All things happen in the inner world long before they happen outside. Anything happening in the external world happened long ago in the internal world. You should know that it happened within you long before it happened outside you. You can know all things that will happen in your future—but you do not. You do not cultivate an understanding. If you concentrate and watch silently, you can know what is going to happen to you in the future—but your mind remains busy in the material world; it has formed the habit of going to the objects that are changing, so it does not notice those subtleties that are received in the inner world.

All things happen in your mental world first. Whether it involves your relationships in your external world, your body, or anything else, it happens first in the mental world. Everything happens in the subtle world long before it take place externally. If you know how to, you can take precautions. The same rock that you trip on can be used beautifully on the front wall of your house or as a stepping-stone. It depends on how you use it. When we can fathom all the subtle levels of life within and reach that spot that is free from all fears, pains, and miseries, then we find ourselves one with the Infinite, where there are no fears, no questions, no problems, no sadness, no pain, and no misery. The message of the great sages is that we can do this. We have only to decide if we want to listen to the world, which tells us to be passive and pessimistic, or to those who are the great leaders of humanity.

Those fortunate few say something else. They tell us that we can do all this in this lifetime. We should cultivate the firm determination: "I can do it, I have to do it, I will do it." Then, when we make our best human effort, all the power within rises, the descending force also blesses us, and grace dawns. Then, at last, we are liberated.

Do not postpone your enjoyment to a future time. What will happen in the next moment of life no one knows. The mystery of life and death is not revealed to everyone; no one has a bag of enlightenment to distribute. If you want to make progress, then do your practice. Your mind raises obstacles, however: "I don't have enough time" or "I don't have enough energy" or "I haven't the means" or "I have no confidence." The answer to all these obstacles is the same: practice and philosophy. Both must go hand in hand. Make a determination, make a resolution, to devote only ten minutes regularly for one month, no matter what happens, and you will begin to see progress.

When you sincerely tread the path, you will meet one who can help you with all setbacks. If you are practicing, I am obliged to attend you, to help, and to serve you. If you are not practicing, then I am not responsible for you. That is my commitment to you. If you are practicing, I am fully prepared to teach, travel, and help you. If you are not practicing, your writing to me or remembering me is of no importance. My duty to you comes only when you are practicing.

A student always wants to examine his teacher. The teacher has to prove that he is a real teacher his whole life. The student always tests the teacher and wants to know that. No matter how many times the teacher proves that he can help you, that he is selfless, you still wonder, "How do I know?"

Students ask their teachers what results the methods will have, where the path will lead, and what difficulties there are on the path. But really, you have to train yourself. You are beginning to grasp things, but you are not honest enough with yourself to follow the path. But there is no other way that you can be transformed.

A teacher and a tradition can help you to go halfway. Learn to apply the other fifty percent of your will to learn what you want to know. Students do not want to use their own free will, but they want someone else to use his will for them. You are complete and have your own power. You have to learn to use that.

If the teacher says not to do something, then a modern student will definitely do it and injure himself. If you do not want to experience something adverse as far as practice is concerned, you will have to listen to those who have already trodden the path, because they have firsthand experience. You do not taste arsenic in order to analyze it;

a scientist always analyzes it in other ways in the lab and then shares his experience with others. The role of the teacher is to offer you systematic and practical methods. Your relationship with the teacher makes you responsible to do your practice. But usually students do not practice, and the teacher becomes disappointed because of that. Those who love their teacher do their practice. Those who do not practice may claim to love, but they do not really love the teacher. The teacher loves the student by imparting the wisdom that was passed on by the great sages.

You are all flowers. Before the petals of the flower of life fall into decay and destruction, offer yourself to the nature to which a child belongs, and enjoy seeing it wherever it is. The teacher also wants you to give a love offering, and that is practice. If you do not practice, you do not love your teacher. In this book I will impart many techniques selflessly and honestly. I am only a messenger; I do not consider myself a sage or anyone special. My duty is to give you the correct message, the way it was transmitted to me; I should transmit it to you in that same manner. If you are eager to learn, you will practice.

On the spiritual path the relationship between the teacher and the student is something very delicate. The quality of the teacher is a very special thing: he is a symbol of selfless service; he is an instrument, a messenger who imparts knowledge without any coloring. A student is one who is prepared to receive the knowledge and who then practices it. But we need to carry our understanding into practice. There is a wonderful quotation from a French writer that states, "A good thought, a great thought, that is not brought into action is either treachery or abortion." You do that to yourself—you become treacherous by not allowing your good thoughts to come into action. You do not allow self-expression in the right way. The main cause of your suffering is not due to heaven, but rather due to yourself through your deeds. The day that you finally understand that you have to work with yourself, that will be a day of accomplishment. A time finally comes when you examine the realities of the world, when you examine the life of the temporal plane, and feel, "I've wasted my whole life. Let me go to the Himalayas; let me go to a monastery; let me go to a sage." Then you will walk toward the goal like you really understand.

CHAPTER TWO

Death and Transition

*T*HE FEAR OF DEATH is one of our most prominent fears. We are all afraid of the word "death" and do not want to face the truth that we all have to die. Why do we fear dying? Death itself is not painful; only the fear of death is painful. When we take off an old shirt to put on a new one, we do not feel fear or pain; we are only pleased to have a new shirt. But the thought of taking off our body brings fear.

This is the way of the world. You see a child dying, an old woman or old man dying, your friend dying, or perhaps sometimes a young, healthy person dying, and you say, "I don't believe in God!" But this is not God's doing. Death has never given you any assurances or guarantees; it comes at any time. And so we fear it. That fear is projected in many ways. Because you see death all around, you worry: "My husband will die—My mother will die—What will happen to me?" You remain constantly insecure. You need to examine that insecurity; you have to understand it and not be afraid. You are sure to die. Even the strongest dies; the best, the most powerful person dies—even a sage dies, although he has a better dying. How can you ignore this reality? Why do you not understand it?

If you merely remember fear, it will create more fear. But if you systematically analyze your fear, you will see that it has a dual face: you are either afraid of losing something, or you are afraid of not gaining something. That is fear. A major fear with each of us is that our body will perish. But you have not analyzed this fear. Would you want your body to be eternal?

There was once a sage who prayed and prayed for eternal life. Finally, God came down and told him, "Okay, go to the spring in that mountain, drink the perennial water, and you will become immortal." So the sage rushed there with great pride and anticipation. But when he thrust himself forward to drink from the water, he suddenly heard many semi-immortal beings shouting to him: "Don't do it! Don't drink the water! We all drank it and we are suffering." So the sage asked, "What's the matter?" They answered, "We wasted our entire energy asking God for eternal life, and God told us to drink the water. Now we are immortal—but to be an immortal human being is not a pleasant thing to be. It is torture being here in this world for a long time. Neither the mind nor the body can handle eternal life."

If we know something about the philosophy of death and the technique of dying, then our fears about death will be eliminated and we will approach death differently. Actually, there is no mother who can give you the shelter that death can. Your physical mother gives you birth; but death gives you real solace and rest. Death is an extension and an expansion of sleep.

In Sanskrit, death is called *sahodara*, or "sister." These two sisters, sleep and death, are born from the same mother, the same source. Just as sleep gives you peace, so also does death give you peace. Sleep relieves you from certain stresses, but death relieves you from the stress of a lifetime. Death puts you into a long sleep. You may sleep now for three hours, but death puts you into a sleep of a hundred years, or perhaps two hundred years. How can we say that death is terrifying? Why do we say that? Why do we not think that sleep is terrifying? We want to sleep; should we also not want to die? But because people are afraid of the subject, there are very few experiments conducted on death.

Instead of avoiding the thought of death, it is very helpful for us to understand what death is. None of us experiences the reality of our death in our daily life. We do not really believe that we will die, although we see others die. There is a constant battle in the human mind and heart about death, but you do not discuss it because you are afraid. So you push aside the fear of death, the highest fear, and then that fear is projected in many ways. You worry that your spouse or father will die, and wonder what will happen to you. Or you worry that your lover will die, or your bank book will die, because you see death all around. This means that you always remain insecure, and you need to examine that insecurity. You have to understand this fear and not be afraid. You are sure to die.

Actually, nobody is really afraid of death—people are afraid of pain and illness. It is a terrible thing when one suffers great pain and does not die. The actual experience of death is not the pain that makes you cry. But if you understand what that suffering is, it goes away. You understand, by that time, that there is no pain in death. Then you are very close to the Reality, though you are not yet enlightened.

Every day you see people leaving you and you call it death, but I do not call it death. I call it merely a parting. Parting is also a great day of meeting. When we part from here, we meet someone else in another place. Where does water go? Let water flow anywhere and finally it will return to the source of all other waters. You also will go toward your own origin.

According to yogic philosophy, death is merely a habit of the body. It is such a deep-rooted habit that one cannot eliminate it. It is very important for you to understand your habit patterns, because your personality is composed of your habits. Thus, if you really want to change your personality, you must learn how to change your habit patterns, transforming your character and your personality.

But what about the habit of death? How can we change death? Is it even possible? Those great, accomplished yogis who live beyond the mundane, and who have devoted their whole lives, all their time and energy, to understanding and analyzing such subjects, know that there is a way. In advanced yoga manuals the technique is called *para-kaya pravesha:* the science of consciously dropping a body and getting into another body. This was such a fascinating subject to me that I thought of devoting my whole life to it. I followed this path very seriously, but not blindly. With all respect and reverence to my master, I always argued with him and questioned why something happened. I knew that certain things did happen, but I wanted to know why. He always said, "I will tell you only by demonstration." He always demonstrated everything, even the philosophical aspects of life.

There is a book titled *The Tibetan Book of the Dead.* It is actually a small part of a larger text that was composed at Nalanda University only about 850 or 900 years ago. It was written by the then Tibetan Prime Minister, who learned Buddhism in India, and brought the knowledge to Tibet. The ideas in that book come from the *Guru Purana*, which is one of the scriptures of the ancient Hindus. The Puranas are explanations of the Vedic rituals, hymns, and sayings, but they are not fully understood because their language is ornamental and sometimes exaggerated in form. To those who are trained, however, the understanding of these texts comes through direct, firsthand experience.

Most of the time you rely on knowledge that is actually imparted by others, and not derived through direct experience. Consider what happens from the very beginning of your life: your mother, your father, your brothers and sisters, your environment, schools and colleges, your country, and the whole of humanity teach you, through many different means. But what is your direct personal knowledge? If what you learn comes only from information received from others, then according to the sages you do not really have knowledge. True knowledge is something else.

The *vidya*—knowledge—that is called *paravidya*—"knowledge beyond"—has nothing to do with *aparavidya* (normal worldly knowledge), but both are necessary and important. Aparavidya is the knowledge of this shore; paravidya is the knowledge of the shore beyond. So there is the knowledge of this shore of life, and there is also the knowledge of the other shore. There is also a third vidya that examines the stage in between both of these and discusses what happens during the transition from one shore to the other. You know something about aparavidya, the techniques and the knowledge of the world, but you do not know anything about paravidya, although you can know it intellectually. You also need to learn about the state called the transition.

Ordinary people die and they do not ever try to understand the mystery of birth and death—the word "death" is terrifying, unknown, and unexplained. What actually happens to you when you die? Who will lead you when you are not able to walk? You have the sense that somebody very dear, very close to you—your beloved husband, your beloved father, brother, or mother—is waiting there to be with you and to help you, but you cannot talk. At the time of transition you cannot communicate with them: you cannot speak, you cannot see; your eyes do not move, your lips do not open. So how do you help yourself at that time?

No matter where you think you will go afterwards, the time of transition itself is very important. Yet you are not preparing yourself for it. Here we are not speaking of reincarnation, which is a different subject, but of the transition immediately after death. You want to know what happens after you drop the body, how you should go, and how you should drop the body. It is important to understand these things. Just as it is important for you to be born into the world, so is it important to know how to leave it. Your mother and father and doctors take care of you and prepare you for life, but no one prepares you for the transition, because no one knows how to do so. A spiritual teacher, however, can quietly prepare you for this transition and give you freedom from the fear of death. A teacher will show you how to drop your body exactly as you take off a garment.

Now, if someone pushes me and I fall, perhaps my garment will be torn and I will feel pain. I may be very much attached to this garment, but if it is worn out or torn it is of no use, it is no longer a means for my evolution. It has become a burden to me, the nation, the world, and all of humanity. The body is weak, decays, and goes to decomposition. So death uses its power over the garment at that time. Death comes and snatches the body. During these final moments such a body needs to be cast off, but consciously. If you know how to consciously take off the garment of your body, then death actually has no power over you.

When the mind is made inward and one-pointed it is possible for a yogi to consciously drop his body willfully. How is it done? There are nine gates in the human body, the city of life, and the tenth is the fontanelle. We find that when the *pranas* depart through the mouth, nose, ears, or any other of the nine gates, that particular part becomes distorted. Yogis practice stillness and lead their pranas through the fontanelle. They do not fear the so-called death. They know what is going to happen to them after they cast off their body. For them death is not a mystery, but is like other changes that occur in life.

We are each attached to our body, even when it becomes torn and old. There is a story about the sage Narada that illustrates how attached we are to our mortal self and to those we love.

Sometimes in the old days children did not care for their parents. Such was the case of the great sage Narada. One day Narada heard his children saying, "Our father is too old. It would be better if he dropped his body—he's suffering."

Narada was very sad to hear this. He helped give birth to those children and he had brought them up, but now they did not want him to live in the world because he was old. So he prayed to God, "Lord, send me Death. This world is so treacherous! I am old; I don't have much energy; I cannot move well. I've brought up these children but they don't care for me. They wish me to die, so please send Death to me."

So Death came to Narada, wearing a long black robe. When Narada saw him, he suddenly asked Death to wait. So Death said, "You are a very good man. You remember the Lord's name all the time. You lived in the world yet remained unaffected, staying above it. What else do you want? Tell me what your wishes and desires are and I'll fulfill them."

So Narada said to Death, "My oldest son is not yet married. Let him get married and then I'll go with you." Death replied, "Okay, so be it. You will have a very good daughter-in-law."

And when the son married, the daughter-in-law had compassion for the old man and began looking after him. But Narada's son did not like that. He said to his wife, "You don't give enough time to me. What have you to do with this old man?"

After some time Narada had a grandson, which greatly pleased him. Again Death came to him, saying, "Now it is time for you to go. Your request has been filled."

But again Narada requested a favor: "Give me some more time so that I can play with my grandson. I want to have him in my lap." Death asked, "How much time?" Narada requested one year and was given it. When the year was completed, he was playing ball with his little grandson when suddenly Death arrived. This time Narada did not even greet him properly. He said, "Why have you come?" Death answered, "I have come to take you with me."

Narada responded, "I don't want to go." He always knew that one day he would have to leave, but his attachment to life had grown so deep that he had forgotten this truth. Death returned to remind him of it.

Death said, "You have been praying for death! What's the matter? Let's go. Your son got married, you have a grandson, you have everything you asked for! Now it's time to go."

But Narada said to Death, "I am playing with my grandson right now. You can take my baggage, but I'll come later on."

So you can see from this story that our attachment to life goes on growing. Your desires are never fulfilled. Desires are the fuel in the fire that you create. Attachment is a worldly necessity; you cannot easily avoid it. A time should come, however, when you should decide that you have done your duties and you have received all the things that you needed in your life. You needed a woman, and you got one. She became your wife and gave you children. Your children have grown up, and now their children are also grown. Your life may be complete, but still human attachment grows and grows and grows. Actually, what should grow is spirituality, not attachment. But, rather than spiritual nonattachment, our attachment grows and then it becomes misery and pain. Attachment, we know, is the mother of misery.

The greatest of all attachments, however, is not toward the people whom you love. That which is most beloved to you is your own self—but since you do not really know that self, you mistake the body for the self and then become attached to it. You are always afraid for your body; you fear that something will happen to it. You do not worry that something will happen to your mind and spirit, yet you constantly wonder what will happen to your body. That fear in your mind creates a pain that is imaginary, but which has immense power because it is never analyzed. So you remain under the pressure of that great pain and those intense fears. You grow with fears. No one, neither a psychiatrist nor a psychologist, can help you with it—not even your teacher. You will have to help yourself by learning to understand that this body is but a habit, and that habit needs transformation.

You are all friends of your bodies. If you calculate, you will find that from morning till evening, ninety-five percent of your time and attention goes toward either your body or someone else's body. When you talk of love, you talk of body love. Even when somebody who is higher and more evolved tells you he loves you, you think that he is talking about your body. You wonder if someone will love you if you become fat or if you lose weight. You always think about your body; your love is limited to it. This shows that the body is what you really love. You have become a lover and your body has become your beloved. All day and night you talk, live, and earn for your body. If ten people say that you are beautiful, then that body gets puffed up with pride. But the body is frail and weak. It is the weakest part of you. It changes, it decays, it feels pain, it goes toward death. And all these pains are transmitted from your body to your brain and then to your mind.

If the scriptures say that the body is like a garment, then how could it not be true? Why do all the scriptures, whether Christian or not, say one and the same thing—that you are not the body? Once, when Christ was crossing a river, he explained this to his disciples, but they did not understand. They said, "Master, you are speaking in a language that we do not understand." But Christ told them that the soul is immortal while the body is mortal and subject to change. The disciples, however, did not understand his language. In our tradition you are taught to drop your body consciously. I have seen the deaths of five people in my tradition, and they all dropped their bodies consciously. Other people there witnessed the deaths as well. It is written, "If you are not able to consciously drop your body, you don't belong to our tradition." In childhood, the first thing a mother teaches a young child is how to put on clothes and how to take them off. The first thing a lover wants is for his woman to take off her clothes. And the first thing that the Great Beloved, Death, teaches us is how to take off the garment of our body.

You can philosophize about death, you can analyze it, and you can practice. In practicing you can learn how to drop your body consciously. Just as your mother teaches you how to take off your shirt and change into another shirt, so you can change your body. You will have to train yourself for this. First you need to learn how to separate yourself from your inner self consciously, and how to come back.

Most people do not believe that a man can consciously drop his body and come back to the body. But if you can consciously wear your garment, then you can also consciously cast it off. This is not a myth. The technique teaches you to separate your senses from your mind, to separate your body consciousness and mental consciousness, and then you are there. But to do this, you have to first learn more basic practices. Unfortunately, you practice for only a few days, then become excited about other things and forget your practice. Your duty to do practice is higher than anything else, but you forget your duty because you have not formed a deep-rooted habit. There are other deep-rooted habits that do not allow you or your mind to go to the new grooves that you are making. At the time of death there are certain sounds, syllables, and words that are used. Throughout your whole life you may have remembered the Lord's name, but suddenly at the end of life your mind fails and you forget everything.

I once saw a woman who was dying. I wanted to help her, so I said, "How are you?" She answered that she was in great pain. So I said, "Say 'Ram, Ram.' Say the Lord's name." The woman said, "How can I say that? I am full of pain!" I answered, "Just say it once!" But she said, "It is not possible. I am in pain." She would not say a small word, but she would say a long sentence! For half an hour I tried to persuade her to say God's name, but she refused. She said only, "You are being funny. I can't say it. I am in pain."

That is called resistance. She, like many of you, resisted the idea of death. You have been negative and passive throughout your life, so even at the end you resist. You are so attached to your body that you cannot think of anything but the body. Yet even in pain the body can be made to exist without sensitivity. If you are in pain, just decide you are not the body, that you are not attached to it, and you will not feel pain.

Breath has a very close relationship with death. As long as you breathe you are alive, but when you stop breathing you are dead. When your body is dropped, what happens? You do not breathe any longer, and without breath you cannot think. When the body is dropped there is no longer a conscious mind, but the unconscious mind remains with you. Your unconscious mind then becomes your vehicle. How do the conscious and unconscious minds work? If I look at you, a sensation goes to my nervous system, my brain, and then to my conscious mind. If I turn my face away to the other side and stop seeing you, why do I remember you? Because the impression is already there in my unconscious mind; you are there. In this same manner, you have billions and trillions of impressions in your mind. Some of the impressions are like bubbles. Some of the impressions are very deep. You see your mother again and again, so your love for your mother is great. That impression is the strongest in your heart and mind. Later you live with another woman. In the beginning you were strangers, but after seeing each other again and again and again, the partner's impression also becomes very strong. Such an impression is called a *samskara*.

When the conscious mind and this mortal body depart, another unit still remains. It is the unconscious mind. The dead body is burned or buried. If you have too much attachment to the body when it is destroyed, then the unconscious unit hovers in the world. "Hey, what happened to my body? What happened to those people whom I love? They do not care for me. I am dead. How sad it is. I did so much for them and they do not care!" The unconscious mind works in this way because you have desires to fulfill. Those desires become your motivation, and they eventually bring you back to this world again. The length of time that it takes for you to come back and put on another garment depends upon your desire. If you have a strong desire to do something, and you could not do it before, then that desire pulls you back.

Sometimes one has a deep impression in the present from the previous life. Your desires can tell you when you will leave and when you will come back. This life is all your determination, your choice. When you are born, you and your parents both choose each other. A child's birth is chosen not just by his parents, but also by himself. So do not blame God. You are not pushed back into this world; you come back to fulfill your desires.

As we said earlier, in this wheel of life you gained a certain status and became a human being. Now it depends upon you what you do. Do you want to go back to a state of unconsciousness, which is hell, or do you want to go forward to enlightenment? Do you want to remain as a human? What happens to you depends on your choice. Nobody creates your destiny. You create it yourself. You can be helped and you can also be tossed around in life's whirlpool. The question is, which do you want?

Desire is stronger than death. One of our strongest desires is love. Love can be experienced on four levels. When love goes to the deepest level it actually becomes treacherous. Then, you cannot live without it because it is with you all the time. If your love is only on the physical level, then you can get another body as the object of your love. If your love is on the mental level, you can also think of another body to love. But if your love goes to the soul level, and you become what in the West is called a "soulmate" to another, then it becomes very difficult. Even for great men who are enlightened, it becomes very difficult. Great men and great angels always go to good people. Like attracts like; water finds its own level. Sometimes, no matter how many children someone has, his love for one particular child will be greater than the love for any other. They will not need to speak of this love, for it is on a very deep level. Sometimes you meet people from the past, and sometimes you meet new people and develop attachments to them. This happens every day. But all these strong desires reside in the unconscious and will pull us back to this plane.

If you analyze your desires in this world you will notice that the desires that remain unfulfilled create frustration. If your desires are not fulfilled, you get frustrated and angry. If there is some desire left in you when you leave this platform, you will come back again to fulfill it, in exactly the same way that you start your day every day. You come to this platform and go away again because of your desires. So you have to analyze and understand your desire-world, so that you can reduce your desires. You should fulfill the important desires that are helpful to you and not fulfill those that are not helpful. It is those unfulfilled desires that bring you back. It is anger that brings you back. Your mind asks, "Why is my body being taken away from me? What is this death? What power has death got? She has great power? Well, I have certain desires to fulfill!"

But then death says, "If your desire is fulfilled, then another desire comes, and there is no end to them." You go on putting fuel in the fire of your desires, but there is no end. It is a constantly burning, unflickering fire, and you are in it. How do you stop it? How do you deal with it?

Great people like Gandhi say that desire is the source of every problem—but there is a shortcut: reduce all your desires, make your desire zero, and you are free. But how difficult that is! The great sages explain that the conscious mind is just a small part of the mind. It is not the entirety of the mind; a vast part of the mind remains sub-merged. That part is the subconscious or unconscious mind. To be unconscious means that we are not aware of something, but it also gives us hope that we can become aware of it. The sages explain that if we learn to expand this conscious mind and make it one, then all knowledge is at our disposal. That is called the method of expanding the conscious mind. The field of the conscious mind is small, but it can be expanded.

However, many problems arise when you try to learn the philosophy of expansion, for instead you have been practicing the philosophy of contraction throughout your life by thinking, "This is mine, this is mine, this is mine!" You have become very small, increasingly going toward contraction. In your life there are two whirlpools: the world manifested by God, and the world created by you. The world created by you is the mind. When you use the word "mine," discriminating between "mine" and "thine," such as by thinking "my home, my wife, my children, my wealth, my prestige, and my ego," you strengthen your sense of "I." That is a mental habit. You are strengthen-ing the vibration by repeating and repeating "I." That is why traditionally one is not allowed to say "I." On this path, the sense of "I-ness" is called "ignorance." By tak-ing off the shackles and barriers of "I" we are walking on the path. The *Yoga Sutras* tell us to eliminate obstacles and barriers. Yet we create this barrier out of insecurity. So there are two philosophies and approaches to life: expansion and contraction. Do you want to follow the philosophy of contraction, or that of expansion?

If you follow the path of expansion, you can go to that state of mind where you can see how your body is dropped. In that state you are legally dead, yet you are still alive. You know that you know the techniques and so you are not afraid of death. You can learn to do that in this lifetime by working with the mind and meditation. You can practice the technique called "expansion." It comes to you when you go into deeper states of meditation. When you go beyond the conscious mind, then you next go beyond the unconscious mind, and then you are in the place of expansion. Before you attain the fourth state of consciousness, *turiya*, the state beyond, you have to go through that state of expansion. That is why the great sages always know the technique of dropping the body. People of God who are conscious and who are aware of the truth know this technique, and drop their bodies intentionally at a specific time.

We will return now to the transition itself. There are two words that are used to describe ways of dropping the body: conscious, and unconscious. If I drop some physical object, I can do so in three ways. First, if someone pushes me and dislodges the thing I hold, then it drops. Secondly, I can drop it unconsciously because I do not have control. Finally, I can drop it consciously. Thus, when you use the words "drop the body," it can mean an act of will or an act out of your control. That is why the sages do not use the word "drop" to describe their departure, just as they do not use the word "death." We use the phrase "cast off the body." This means to consciously change the garment. The garment is now dirty or full of holes, it is torn or it is not suitable to your age and time. It is no longer a means for you; it does not protect you; it is not appreciated by others; it does not help you. It has actually become a source of problems for you. So, then, the teacher will tell you to cast off your body, to change your garment. This means that you have the will to do it.

The Sanskrit word for this, *mukti*, means that one has attained the final liberation. There are three categories of beings passing through this camp: those whose death is uncontrolled, those who die consciously, and those who are *amara*, or eternal. The first category of beings are mortals who do not know what is best in life or what death is, so they die like other creatures in the world. They are not controlled by nature, but they are controlled by their own uncontrollable nature, which they have created. These people die because they do not know any other way. They are born to die. And if you are born to die, you do not like to be born. That is a fact.

The second category of people who die leave their body consciously. They even tell their close students that they will cast off their body on such and such day and time. Casting off their body remains under their conscious will. Death has no access to such yogis and enlightened souls.

The third category, those who are eternal, we should not bring down to the category of human beings. But because a human being can also attain eternity here, we can call them human beings. They are attained, yet they walk with us. They are born with us, yet they have attained eternity. There are a fortunate few great people who come to the earth, walk on the earth, live like us, and do as we do. Yet they remain unattached because they know that they have come on a definite purpose and journey, and are merely passing through this camp.

This third category of people say that death is as natural as birth. They are called the amara. Just as birth is a habit of the body, they also see death as a habit of the body. Many people have the idea of controlling death, but they do not know how to do so. The amara have learned to control it. These amara, who are eternal, are *avadhutas* and *muktas*—free souls—on the earth. They have the capacity to lead people. They lead them and then go away. In all traditions there are some people of this level. They find pleasure in casting off the body, in changing the garment, because they know that when this garment is useless, another garment will be better. They change the garment willfully, knowingly, and consciously. The amara truly have victory over death. The amara say it is best to live long so that we can achieve the goal of life. Ignorant people say, "We are helpless, we don't know anything, so let us eat, drink, and be merry." The amara say, "No, we have to fulfill our purpose"; they enjoy both the world and eternity—*bhukti* and *mukti*, respectively. They say that this can be done, that it can be done in this lifetime, if you remember and remain aware of your goal of life. But you have to understand the goal.

What will happen to us after death? We all wonder about this. We wonder if heaven and hell are real places. Hell and heaven are not really explained in any culture because that would require another huge Bible! According to the philosophy of this tradition, one does not live in hell or heaven after death. Who experiences hell and heaven? The body and breath do not experience hell and heaven. It is that unique experience called the individual soul, the unconscious mind, that experiences them. That particular unit of soul and unconsciousness is what you call in English, "spirit." The soul is pure; it is our essential nature; it is pure *atman*. You are inside a vehicle, the *jiva* that experiences pain and pleasure. The jiva is the union of atman and the unconscious mind.

The atman and the *para-atman*, the Absolute Reality,

are essentially one and the same, identical. A drop of water is the ocean; a seed is a tree. There is no difference. If you analyze a drop of water and the ocean, there is no difference. Qualitatively, there is no difference; quantitatively, there is a difference. Our atman is the same as the para-atman, that Absolute Reality, qualitatively. It is our mind that measures quantitative things. That great majesty of atman lives and dwells in our own being and also in the smallest particle. He is great because He has the capacity to be in the smallest microscopic entity, and also lives in the greatest. He is great because He lives in both the smallest particle and in the greatest particle. He is great, but He is not beyond your reach.

The jiva is a vehicle full of memories, desires, and wishes. Atman, when linked to the unconscious mind is called the jiva. Without the unconscious mind you are pure atman, and when you realize that you are pure atman, you are also para-atman. That is called *moksha*, or liberation. The moment you realize that this is your essential nature, that you are pure atman, you are free.

The first freedom comes when you "realize" this— when you experience it, not when you merely analyze it intellectually. You may analyze this philosophically, but that analysis does not help you without actual realization. The union of the unconscious with the atman makes you jiva. If the vehicle of the jiva is not there, you are called atman. When you realize that you are identical with the para-atman, that you are a wave of bliss in the ocean, playing in the ocean, and remaining there, then you are eternal, you are free, you are para-atman.

When this occurs you have not lost your identity; you still have your individual identity. You are a nucleus and this universe is your expansion. You are not merely a part of the universe. By thinking that you are only a part of the universe you become very small, you reduce yourself to dust. Rather, this universe is your expansion. Para-atman is the expansion of atman. Atman is not a mere part of Brahman. It is not just a small spark. Atman cannot be diminished. You are essentially atman, but you need expansion into para-atman. You need to realize this, and not merely through mental analysis. To realize this you have to practice, and to practice you have to understand what creates problems for you and what becomes obstacles in your life. Of course there are hell and heaven, but what type of hell and heaven are they? There is the present hell, which you have created for yourself. Hell is whenever your mind is not clean, when it is made gross by *tamas* or negativity, when you have lost the faculty of discrimination. You think that the things of this world are better than hell, but this world is a living hell. Every individual makes hell for himself.

There is no place on the other side of death where you are punished if you are a bad person or if you have committed a crime. Of course you are punished, but you are punished here. You are punishing yourself wherever you go, whether you come here or go somewhere else, because wherever you go, your mind goes with you.

The Sanskrit texts emphasize love, knowledge, and attainment. The knowledge of the world is that everything is subject to change. Today you call something beautiful and wonderful; tomorrow it can become ugly. Those who are loving can learn to hate you. That which you think is yours can be separated from you. A father and son both know that the day will come when they will leave each other. They know it, but they do not want to face it. No one knows who goes from this plane first. A father or son can make all kinds of sacrifices and still know that a day will come when they will suffer because they part. They suffer because they forgot; they pushed the idea aside. They did not analyze or understand this, and that is why they are suffering. Suffering means ignorance. Suffering is not self-existent; it is a result of your ignorance. To know your final goal is to finally leave behind the world of suffering.

· CHAPTER THREE ·

Transforming Negative Thought Patterns

*T*he sages say that the only difference between you and them lies in the nature of your thoughts and your mind. If someone tells you that you are bad or have done something wrong you accept it, and you become bad. If you even think it, then you feel bad. You cannot forget that thought. You want to forgive yourself, but you have a habit of retaining such negative thoughts. Some people retain good and helpful thoughts, and others retain negative and passive thoughts. That is why the view of yoga is that those thoughts that are helpful should be encouraged, and those thoughts that are not helpful should not be encouraged. On the path of meditation you learn this process.

Suppose a thought comes into the mind that you should slap someone. The faculty of discrimination can tell you that it is not a good thing to do, and then the thought will diminish. An ordinary man retains the negative thought, while a sage allows it to pass away.

There is one issue that is very practical and concrete, and you should remember it if you really want to practice meditation. Often a thought comes into your mind and you become absorbed by that thought because of your habits and lack of training. Then, after a few minutes or hours, you suddenly wake up; you wonder what has happened and why this thought has controlled you. You need to practice to be free from the strong grip of those thoughts that do that to you. If one thought comes and then another thought comes, and if this continues indefinitely, then what becomes of your mind?

Then your mind is a catalog of thoughts, which include desires, wishes, and wants, and you can put them into various categories, such as inclinations or sensations. You can certainly create a hell that way! Every individual makes hell for himself. You create hell wherever you go, because wherever you go, your mind goes with you. As we said earlier, the world created by you is the mind. When you use the word "mine" and emphasize your individual identity, you strengthen your sense of "I." That is a mental habit: you strengthen that vibration by repeating and repeating "I." But this sense of "I" is ignorance; it is what keeps you from expanding your sense of self. By taking off this shackle and barrier for yourself, you are beginning to understand your essential nature. You create this barrier of the ego out of insecurity.

But human beings have a tendency to blame others for their difficulties; first of all they blame nature, and then finally, God. They do not want to take the responsibility themselves. They do not think, "If I am ignorant, why should God be responsible for my ignorance?" Most human beings do not think that. If you are suffering, why should others be responsible for your suffering? In reality, you are the sufferer; you created suffering for yourself. When you take this sort of responsibility—the moment you understand that—you gain a new courage, and it is a courage and strength that you need.

At the lowest level of the human mind you have ignorance; then at the next stage you have control plus knowledge; and finally you have the perfection to be with the Eternal. Then that absolute Reality or eternity assigns you jobs. Do not think that you are presently assigned to a job: you are presently assigned to suffer, because you have assigned it to yourself. But at the highest level of human development, the sages see that human beings are not utilizing the eternal wisdom. They come to this plane and teach and suffer. The great people, like Christ, Krishna, Moses, and Buddha—all those people who led the masses and whom still today the masses love, respect, and follow—have come from the Source, from eternal infinity.

Even those in ignorant states of mind can attain this. There is always a chance. Why do you want to do something today? Analyze your feelings: do you create an entirely new atmosphere today? The reason you want to wake up in the morning is that you want to complete that which is incomplete from before, from yesterday. In the same way, you are born to complete the task that you have assigned to yourself, so you try to complete it. Whether you can actually complete it or not in this life is a different question. But you came to this plane because you had a desire to do something; that is why you work.

But something else happens to us in this world. We use so much time and energy merely for our physical being that we do not have time for our higher knowledge, for our attainment. We go on collecting and gathering desires, and finally we become full of desires. Everybody is overburdened with many, many desires. You are all under stress because of your desires. It is not that God wants to punish you; you punish yourself and then you ask God to help you.

The Upanishads say: "Wake up! You are in a state of deep sleep, the sleep of ignorance. You can become free of these desires, ignorance, and misery; you can understand your real goal and your essential nature."

If you understand only these issues—ignorance, death, meditation, and samadhi—everything will be revealed to you. No book can go beyond this. And even if you read the best of the books, they do not explain enough on the subject. Or if the writers really understand it themselves, there is no power in words to explain certain things. You cannot explain certain things with words. If I have pain, I can only say that I have pain, but you do not feel it. If I am eating something sweet and I say that it is great, I still cannot convey the taste. That is my experience; we all have to take responsibility for ourselves first.

It is not possible for you to abandon this work and this world, because you have assigned yourself duties. The call of duty is higher, definitely, because you have to learn to fulfill your duties. You have to find a way of living in the world and, at the same time, being aware of the Ultimate.

But there is another problem: when you try to do this, either you should learn to make this world a means to your goal, or you should renounce the world completely. There is no other way; there are only two paths, actually. The many other paths spring from these two main paths of renunciation or selfless action. It is important that you know this, that you have understood.

On the path of renunciation you renounce the world;

that renunciation may be seen as irresponsibility by the people of the world. But the best of the people of the world renounced the world, because the world did not have the power to retain them. The world did not have anything worthwhile to offer; it could not please them. It tried its best to retain them by offering many charms, temptations, and attractions, but after analyzing the things of the world, they did not become attached. Nonattachment is needed both in the world and outside the world. This is one of the essential virtues that you need. The first virtue that you need is love, which means to give without any condition. If there is any condition in your love, that is not called giving; if there is any resistance, that is not called giving; if you are seeking a reward, that is not called giving. The rewards of love come only after you leave this platform, when you are no longer in the world. Do not expect them now. If you are in search of a reward on the path of love, you will never obtain it. That sweet offering of love is a great step, which gives you awareness of another step, another dimension of life.

Another dimension of life can also be analyzed as suffering. You suffer because you are deprived of enjoying the objects of the world. You want to enjoy those things that you consider to be the finest objects in the world— but even if you get what you want, after a few minutes, months, days, or years, you are disappointed. The answer is not in the objects of the world; you know from the very beginning that no object in the world is perfect. Everything is subject to change, death, decay, and decomposition. But you have not developed your understanding; you have not examined it from all sides. When you develop that understanding, then you are nonattached—and that nonattachment means love, not indifference. Attachment means misery and pain. Attachment means creating a whirlpool for yourself and preparing yourself to be miserable in the future. You create attachment because the nature of your senses is external. The mind uses your senses to enjoy the world. Those so-called enjoyments are temporal and momentary, and after you have enjoyed them repeatedly, you get frustrated. You expect there to be a higher or better enjoyment that can be obtained from elsewhere. The problem does not lie in the objects that you are enjoying—this is your own problem, because you have not attained the state of mind that comes automatically after serious analysis, observation, and realization. Once you have analyzed this issue, do not think that you have *realized* it yet. You still have to assimilate that analysis.

You have come to accomplish your desires. You do not accomplish them, and so you are reborn again. There is some desire left in you when you leave this platform, so you come back again to fulfill your desires, in exactly the same way that you start your day every day with what was left undone the day before.

Learn to understand this: that you come to this platform and go away because of your desires; and remember that you have to analyze and understand your desire-world. Then you can work to reduce your desires. To achieve this, learn to fulfill those important desires that are helpful to you, but do not fulfill those which are not helpful. Desires will die if you do not allow them to be materialized and fulfilled in the external world.

If you have negative thoughts or desires that are not helpful, remind yourself of your purpose. Tell yourself that this thought or desire is distracting and will lead you to a fantasy. You can philosophize in this way and then you can understand the process and strengthen your practice. If you commit a mistake and are flattened by that mistake, then you usually start condemning yourself; that is not helpful and will make you sick. Presently, you face many problems because you have not trained yourself. The preliminary steps are to watch your gestures and movements and to discipline your body.

We have been discussing the way you create your own misery, but actually, pain is a great thing to experience. No one likes it, but it can give us a great understanding. Whatever creativity I have found in myself, I discovered it because of pain, and it is a joy. That painful joy has led me to write poems, to compose my own songs, to be with myself, and to feel that this world is just a camp; it is not my home. Nothing belongs to me; I have come to serve; I have not come to enjoy the things of the world—that is my philosophy of life. My master tried his best to train me. I am very sensitive, and he could not take away the inherent quality of my soul to be in deep pain and sorrow, disappointed by the world. Many times I examined life, and when I saw someone with that which I thought I wanted, I went to that person and saw that they were not happy, and then I wanted something more from life. The prime desire in life should be to attain a state of enlightenment; then you will never be disappointed.

You should always hang on to one sweet thought: that all the things of the world are only a means. Use these means to attain the end goal of life. If you know how to do this, then you will enjoy having those means. You will not think that you possess them, because they are only a means. Then you will remain nonattached, you will enjoy the means, and you will be loving toward others. You should love whatever means you have. You do not have to be indifferent or cruel toward the means, nor do you have to be attached to them. There are many paths that lead you to the height, to the summit. No path should be condemned; only ignorant people condemn other paths. In both the path of the world—the path of action—and in the path of renunciation, in both these two major paths, you have to be nonattached.

This plane is a well-known ground for our attainment. You have come here to attain something, and on the way toward that attainment you should enjoy your life. All the things of the world are meant for you; so enjoy them, but do not have a feeling of ownership for the things of the world, for they are not yours. You should understand this one principle clearly: since all the things of the world are meant for you, make the best use of them, and make them into means to attain your goal. On the path, enjoy all the means that come your way. Whatever you have, apply it as a means toward the goal. But these objects are only means; do not become attached to them. This world is not yours; it is given to you and you should make the best use of it. You are not the owner of this world, you should not try to possess anything. The feeling of possessiveness is injurious to you. You should be free from this evil of possessiveness, which is very bad for you. This way of thinking should be strengthened, and should become a part of your habit. Then those negative mental habits that have created long, deep grooves in the mind spontaneously go.

For many of you, there is one serious problem in your progress, and that is with the habit patterns that you have formed. Many of your habits you do not like, but you cannot get rid of them because of a lack of practice. You have not made enough effort to get rid of your habits. To do this, you have to repeatedly do something that creates new grooves in your mind, so that your mind stops flowing into the old grooves and starts flowing into the new grooves that you are building. Then your habits are transformed, your personality is being transformed, and your character starts to be transformed. This is the process of transforming yourself. It requires practice!

You become habit-addicted in life; you suffer because of your own habits. It is because of your bad habits that you divorce your wife or husband. The entire world is in the bondage of habit patterns. But habits cannot be merely changed. If you just replace your habit patterns, nothing happens. You should learn to transform your habit patterns. Transformation means that when your mind is going into these old grooves, you change that. How can you transform your habits? Perhaps you think that a swami can do it but that you cannot do it. But I crawled like you; I walked like you; I did many silly things like you. There is a method called transforming the habit patterns—not merely changing the habit patterns. There is a difference between a car and a human being: a human being needs transformation and not a mere change. Your mind needs to be transformed because it causes problems for you rather than helping you toward your goal.

Suppose, for example, that you claim to love someone. When you worry, you do not remember your lover during that time, you remember your worry instead. So which do you really love? You love your worry, because the real object of your thoughts is your worry, not your lover. This means that you love the object of worry more than the person who loves you, because you are helpless, and your mind goes to that groove of worry again and again, and that groove is strengthened by repeatedly doing that. Finally a time comes when the pattern is a mental habit, and then, if it is severe enough, it is called a sickness.

There are patients who cannot be treated by drugs, suggestions, yoga, or any therapy—no matter which therapy you try. Nothing helps such a patient because their mind has formed a habit and that habit deepens into a groove and creates many grooves. Then it is a deep-rooted habit, and you are caught.

The question is how you can come out of these grooves. To become desireless is a very good philosophy. Then, you start creating another kind of groove in the mind. Greatness comes to human beings when new grooves are made in the mind. And you have the power and capacity to start creating new grooves. Then, the mind will sometimes travel here and there because of the old habit, but at the same time you are also creating conscious habits.

Death is not a remedy for these problems you face; it is merely a deep sleep, it gives rest. It is not a process of education. Sleep is not an education; it is essential, but it is only rest. Somehow you have to educate yourself, and there is no other method for self-transformation but meditation. When you meditate, a time comes when the mind stops this negative habit and develops freedom from these old grooves. The first step toward freedom comes when you are able to make new, strong grooves within the mind. This is called real self-transformation; it is not just change.

Individual effort can lead you to a state of happiness and a state of heaven. It is the mind that creates heaven and hell. First, the mind is hopeless and helpless, and says that it cannot deal with the situations of the external world or the inner world. But when you train the mind, then it is led to a state where it has enough fire, warmth, and freedom from all pain and miseries, and it can go beyond. But usually you think only of acquiring things that you do not have. You are tossed about all the time by your mind and its desires. If you go to somebody who has the very object you desire and ask if he is happy, he will say he is not. So what do you really want? The mind goes through the process of examining superficial things and looking for happiness, but it does not find it. You seek to renew your energy in external objects, but they do not inspire you or give you energy. The mind finds real happiness only when it tries to find the source of energy within.

Your mind is in the habit of using the agents called the senses. The moment you wake up in the morning, your mind immediately contacts the senses. You decide to have a cup of tea, so you get up, go to the kitchen, and make a cup of tea. But it does not stop there: you decide to make breakfast, to change your clothes, to prepare for work, and to find your portfolio. Your mind contacts your senses, and the senses always distract and dissipate your energy.

In meditation you do not allow your senses to dissipate your mental energy, because you are sitting and attending within. You can also meditate when you are walking, provided you have practiced and have the capacity and strength not to allow your mind to dissipate your energy. This control, called *tapas*, stops the senses and mind from dissipating your energy. When your senses contact matter you receive two kinds of impulses: one is called pain, and the other is pleasure. When your senses take in a wall, you receive a sensation, and you say it is white, or it is cream-colored. Then, if your mind pays attention, it goes on penetrating and finding out all the details. This is constantly happening. The mind alone has the capacity to work so vigorously. What a wonderful capacity the mind has!

Now suppose you decide to make a tape recording of your mental processes: any thought that comes into your mind, you will let the tape record it. To record five minutes of thoughts you need a whole day; for one day's thoughts, you need a month. The mind works very fast— so you need to learn to calm your mind, to make it one-pointed. For success in either the external world or in the internal world, you need a one-pointed mind.

Presently you do not have a one-pointed mind because you have not learned to tame the senses. If you do not train a dog or cat, it can destroy your home. Similarly, you have to learn to tame the senses, because you cannot work without them. You have to make use of your senses. Instead, you are generally a slave of the senses. One approach to managing the senses is to completely satisfy all your senses, and then the mind can go to a deeper aspect. This is a poetic way, but another method is to disconnect the senses and ask your mind to go beyond them. There are these two alternatives.

Do not forget the goal and become lost in the charms and temptations of the senses. The senses have their place and joy, but do not become absorbed in them. That is not all; that is not everything. You cannot ignore the needs and demands of your body; you need to eat and nourish the body. The body has its needs. But to become lost in the needs of the body, if your nights and days are laden with wants and desires, is not wise. That is not being aware of the Reality.

You can convert all the means you have, all the instruments you have, and all the situations and circumstances of your life into means to attain the goal. This is one path. Another path is to accept things as they are and to learn to make use of the things of the world and yet remain detached. To be detached does not mean to be indifferent; to be detached means to love. The definition of detachment and nonattachment is love, not indifference. If you are detached you can love others well, because you become more objective. You are involved, yet you remain objective. That is the path of nonattachment, and it is higher even than renunciation. If you renounce something but lack nonattachment, that is of no use. First you should learn to grow in nonattachment, and then you are better than a renunciate or a karma yogi, because you have grown. Both paths, the path of renunciation and the path of action, require something called nonattachment—that is, learning how to live in the world and yet remain above and unaffected.

A lotus does exactly that: it grows out of the mud, but it remains unaffected by the mud. This whole world is a muddy swamp, and if you are born in the swamp, you have to learn to live in it. The way to do that is to keep your petals above, unaffected and untouched. That is why the symbol of yoga and meditation is the lotus. Whichever path you take, you must learn to cultivate nonattachment in working with your desires in the world, or you will never be truly satisfied. When you understand the role of the mind and how to properly use the objects of the world, then, like a lotus, you are unaffected and untouched by the world, and you have learned to transform your own mind and personality.

CHAPTER FOUR

Understanding the Mind and the States of Consciousness

*T*HE JOURNEY on which we are now treading and being led is an internal journey, a journey within. On an external journey you move faster and faster until it is complete—but on this journey you do not move, and yet you go ahead. The laws of this internal journey are entirely different. They comprise the science of yoga. You want to be an interior researcher; you want to know something valuable. To do that, the first thing you need to do is to understand the four states of consciousness: the waking state, the dreaming state, the state of deep sleep, and the state beyond.

Once you understand the first three states, then you definitely understand that there is something beyond. The state beyond is not known by ordinary people. But how fortunate is he who touches Infinity while he is here. Even the greatest of people cannot do that. Even those on the other side cannot do that. Even *devas*, or celestial beings, cannot do that. Great is he who lives here, yet remains above. This finite vessel of the body has something great in it: it carries the Infinite all the time. It is a glass box or a glass house in which Infinity lives. All the expressions of your face, all your smiles, have been created by that Great One who peeps through these windows and through the corridor of your life.

Understand one thing first: you should always think that it is easy to meet Him. To speak to others you have to move your lips, but to converse with Him you do not have to do that. You just have to be quiet and silent. You do not have to do any work or take any action to receive great joy. If any such action is performed, it is performed in the inner world in a subtle manner.

We will begin to discuss the waking state, following the teachings of the Upanishads. They are considered to be the finest literature on the best of the philosophies in the world. The Upanishads are the finest part of the Vedas, which are the most ancient scriptures in the library of humanity today. It is not easy to understand them, however. They are composed of *sutras*, or "threads," which are small, compact aphorisms, not easily understood without a teacher.

According to the Upanishads, you first need to understand the waking state and to learn to work with your mind. During the waking state, you remain awake and conscious. The entire educational system, all over the world, has only one thing to teach you: that which applies to the waking state. While awake in the external world, if you learn to coordinate your senses and to establish a coordinated function with that external world, then you are considered to be great.

But in the external world where you live, "wisdom" often means stealing, drinking, being harsh to others, being injurious, being hurtful and harming. This is because you make your own ego the center of your life.

The ego is only meant to be a representative—but that representative, forgetting its true master, starts to function and control things in the external world. Let us see how the ego is used—wisely and foolishly—in the waking state. The purpose of the ego is to hold and retain your body, to retain your individuality. But there is nothing beyond that! As long as the ego is functioning to retain your individuality, it is doing its work well. But unfortunately the ego gets involved with other things, and tries to get involved with others' individuality as well. So if you believe that your partner is superior to you in some regard, you cannot accept that; a struggle goes on, and then the marriage or friendship falls apart.

When this happens, it means the partners have not accepted each other as they are. Then how can they really love? They have accepted each other merely for their own convenience—and to accept someone for one's own convenience is not love, it is selfishness; it is food for the ego.

In the external world, only the ego is strengthened. Whatever we do, we do it for the sake of the ego, and the ego's function is merely to retain this body successfully in the external world. The ego does not know anything important, but if you give all your energy to the ego and go on increasing your ego with all your mind, action, and speech, then you will find that you have become a great ego. With such an ego you build walls around yourself. You share the same bed and the same roof with someone, you love somebody, and you accept them as a partner—and then you build a boundary around yourself and do not allow that person to know how you are feeling inside, and what you are thinking. You cannot share your innermost ideas and feelings, even with yourself.

Therefore the vast portion of your personality remains submerged because of the walls between your ego and you, and between you and the Reality. The vastness of the mind is not known to you and remains forever submerged. What is submerged is the unconscious or subconscious, which then is not understood. Psychologists used this word "subconscious" earlier; in modern times everything is considered to be "unconscious." The unconscious means you own it and you have it within, but you are not aware of it. To bring forward the unconscious wealth that is the infinite library in the mind, you simply have to allow it to come forward. Even meditation will not totally help.

There is another way—the intuitive way of receiving information from the mind. Intuition dawns when you learn to calm your mind. When you calm your mind and when you meditate deeply, your mind becomes one-pointed, free from all other thought patterns. During that time one has the power to penetrate and pierce through those folds of mind that are not ordinarily penetrated by any human being.

A one-pointed mind makes you inward, so you can really start your journey in earnest. You cannot start this journey without a one-pointed mind. To develop one-pointedness, first learn to watch your mind. Sit down and watch how many times your mind becomes distracted. After ten days of practicing this, your mind will become distracted much less often.

Your mind has become a tool that creates bondage for you. You should have a dialogue with your mind as a friend—and do not accept everything it says, because your friend is not perfect. Neither are you perfect—but whatever your mind says, watch. Whatever you say, the mind already watches. The mind depends totally on its previous experiences, and imagines future experiences based on that. You have one goal: you want to experience that which is neither the past nor the future, but now. If you watch your mind, you will see your progress. These are milestones on the path to the royal house that is called samadhi, the highest state of consciousness.

The waking state is actually only a small part of the mind. We do not know how to have access to the entirety of the mind. We do not presently understand how to know the mind in its wholeness. Jesus, Moses, Krishna, and Buddha were born exactly like us, they walked like us, and they died like us, but they became great because somehow they came into contact with the beyond.

The waking state can be expanded. It can become a means for us. Any state of mind—waking, dreaming, or sleeping—can be used as a means to attain the goal. We are talking of the inner world, but the same thing can be applied in the external world. As we discussed, you can convert everything you have—all the instruments you have, all your situations and circumstances—into means to attain the goal. The waking state can be expanded—but even if you do not want to expand it, then you should still learn how to make your mind one-pointed through meditation on a focal point. This requires only a small part of the totality of the mind to bring your waking state into balance. You lead your mind to a state where there is no sound, the place of soundless sound.

When you have attained that state, you cannot believe the joy and the rest you will attain! Do not think that only swamis and yogis can achieve this; everyone can do it. You must only learn to focus your mind.

When you focus your mind in the external world, that

is called "concrete concentration." For concrete concentration you need an object, but that object should not go against your mental tendencies. If you concentrate on your girlfriend whom you love, you will land in bed with her and create a whole distraction for yourself. So the focus of the mind should not be on sensual objects. In concrete meditation or concrete concentration, do not meditate on such objects. You can concentrate on somebody whom you love and respect. However, if your love does not have great respect, do not do that because it is dangerous: your concentration will be sensualized because of it. If you learn to respect the one whom you love, then that person can be used as an object of concentration, using your beloved as an object of concentration in the external world.

While performing your external duties, you can act consciously. You do many things unconsciously, however, merely because they have become habits. You merely react. So you are a reactionary and not a yogi. You are *bhogis*—those who enjoy pleasure—because you are reactionaries. A yogi can be a good bhogi, yet he will still be a yogi; but a bhogi can never be a yogi. Be conscious when you are eating your food. Be silent and pay attention to the type of food it is, its color, how it tastes, and how you are enjoying it. Instead of eating mindlessly while chattering, eat your food consciously. Examine whether it tastes good and whether you like the taste. Learn to see your food, talk to your food, really eat your food—that is the conscious way of eating. In the same manner, have sex consciously and sleep consciously. You rush to bed with your partner in an unconscious habit. The conscious way of doing things is entirely different from acting out one's unconscious habits. The unconscious thoughts are not under your control, and usually you are led blindly by them. Consequently you cannot use the conscious mind, which your whole life you have worked to create and train. And since the conscious mind is only a small part of your mind, you are nowhere, neither in the unconscious nor in the conscious. That is why you are in such turmoil.

The worst aspect of the mind is that it teaches you to lean on something besides the Reality. The mind wants to lean all the time; your mind is never free. You want your mind to be free, but it is never really free. It is always filled with some object, some idea, some thought, or some emotion. This means that the mind always wants to lean or depend on something.

Your mind becomes dependent and passive because in the waking state you receive information through books, through teachers, and through many other channels. Your work is to put it all through your own filter. That filter is time. Often you cannot decide things on time; you are not using your filter. When something comes into your mind you jump up in reaction and do things, but you do not allow your external knowledge to go through that filtration that is already within you. Those who do not use this filter are not successful. Those who do use it are considered to be wise in the world.

Time is the greatest of all filters. Perhaps you are very sad today because you lost something—but after a few days you forget it because you keep yourself busy in other matters. The time span makes the difference; time is a filter that heals, pacifies, and teaches. You should learn to use that filter of mind. Whatever information comes, let it go through the mind. The mind becomes rusty if you do not use it. The faculty of discrimination, *buddhi*, is one of the important faculties of your mind, the *antahkarana*. The mind becomes very sharp and penetrative when you learn to use time's filter consciously. Some people have the capacity to pacify and reassure themselves when something adverse happens, because they use their filter. The filter of time, one of the prime conditioners of the mind, can be used properly. Time is a great therapeutic tool, and when you learn to use it, it becomes one of the most powerful parts of self-therapy.

The mind itself does not do anything directly; it has agents. The mind is very clever. Your body may be prosecuted, but the mind cannot be punished. It may motivate you to commit crimes, yet it is never punished. However, the mind also motivates you to do all the good deeds, and it does not want a reward. So the mind, in its true nature, is actually free from rewards and punishment. The mind is not something bad; it is the finest tool that you can have. You just need to learn to understand it.

Another quality of mind is that it wants to remain busy. The moment it is not occupied, it starts absorbing your power, energy, and interest. Keep the mind free and it will do anything. Once the mind is free from negative thought patterns, you have to direct your mind to certain focal points, according to your tradition. Your mind is in the habit of using the agents called the senses to keep busy.

The mind is always preoccupied with thinking. It never thinks that it is old except when its body does not act according to its wish. What it used to do before, the older body does not do. The mind is never old, but in old age the mind is preoccupied and full of follies. It is best if you know how to direct your mind and make use of it. The best use of the mind is self-training.

Many of you are very bright and wonderful, better than any of your teachers, but you do not have the ability to bring forward the fund of knowledge that you have stored in your unconscious mind. The problem is with the conscious mind that functions during the waking state, and which you use in your daily life. It is considered to be the creative aspect of your life, that which is cultivated and educated. Many of you have wonderful qualities and abilities in your unconscious, but you do not know how to express them. Psychologists have not yet found a way of taming the unconscious, of knowing its vast reservoirs, or tapping the infinite library within. Many desires from your unconscious mind, however, are expressed in the dreaming state.

Dreaming is the second state of consciousness. The dreaming state is therapeutic. You may have a dream that you are with your husband, for example. That dream arises because such a desire was stored in the unconscious. Later, when your conscious mind relaxes, the desire comes forward. That is what creates dreaming.

Therefore, a dream is the result of unfulfilled desires waiting for fulfillment. The dream has the power to pacify you. That is why it is therapeutic. But it is also a disease. Many people dream all the time—this means that they have millions of desires to fulfill and they are not able to fulfill their desires, so they dream. Those who daydream do so because they have expanded their mind but they do not know how to use it. Thus, instead of expanding the waking state consciously with meditation, contemplation, and prayer, their dream state expands. When the dream state expands, it is a waste of time, energy, and human potential. You can easily analyze your dreams: your dreams are your unfulfilled desires, wishes, and wants.

Dreaming is great therapy. If you do not dream, either you are beyond it or you are sick. A dream is a doctor, but that doctor also has limitations. Dreaming cannot cure chronic diseases. If you have a desire left unfulfilled in your mind, when you go to sleep that desire comes forward. All your fantasies and fancies are satisfied and cured by your dreams. Your fantasies and fancies create agitation in the mind—a sickness—and that sickness is cured by your dreams. Sometimes dream analysis helps you understand, but to analyze a dream is also dreaming, because now you are using the waking state for the wrong purpose. You have already dreamed; now why do you want to analyze what you dreamed? You are using precious waking time for the analysis. This means that you want to be in the dream state, you want something again. You want to remain in a state of unfulfillment—that is what your dreams are.

Most of your sleeping time is wasted by your dreams, just as your daydreams waste most of your waking state. Daydreams happen because you have not trained the subtle part of your mind to focus in the external world.

The mind has the capacity to receive hunches, but the mind has no capacity to receive intuitive knowledge. Intuitive knowledge is not received through the mind. The mind itself has only the power to receive hunches, which cannot be relied upon. If a hunch is true once, you still cannot trust the hunch that comes the next day because it may be untrue. The mind has no power to understand, analyze, realize, or know the source of a hunch.

It is similar with prophetic dreams. Sometimes you have prophetic dreams. They mean that your mind has gone beyond time. In deep sleep sometimes you have an intervention through a dream, and when it comes true it is called a prophetic dream. But only that particular type of dream is a prophetic dream. It is important not to create a conflict in your mind. Sometimes a dream comes from your identification with somebody very close to you. Perhaps that person is sick, and you identify yourself with him. One day your mind will feel that you are going to die. This kind of dream is never true. You have to understand and analyze which dreams are accurate and which are not.

You have to examine your dreams. Most dreams are due to your unfulfilled desires, and since a dream is a doctor, the dream treats you. Your desires create a level of disease in you because of your frustrations and suppressions. Many physical frustrations that come about through a relationship or through food or sex will be "treated" by your dreams. Dreams have the power to do that. Perhaps you are unable to have sex because you do not have a partner—you are fussy about it and the potential partners are also fussy, so you are frustrated. Then, the dream is a kind of compensation.

The yogis say that you can analyze the whole universe and know everything about it by understanding yourself and your mind. You have two sides, like a magnetic pole. One side is negative and the other side is positive. In man the positive side is his right, and the negative side is his left; in woman it is reversed. In the center of your spinal column, in the centralis canalis, there are two flows of energy, the *ida* and *pingala nadis*, which are associated with the sympathetic and the parasympathetic systems. You can see how unity and diversity are arranged in a beautiful way. You want to know about the universe—and to know about it, you will have to know the miniature universe that is yourself. You are becoming a scientist, and you want to know about the universe, yourself, your relationship with the universe, and all the mysteries of the universe. You want to learn everything—but to do this you need to understand yourself and your mind first.

Sleep is the third state of consciousness. What happens to your intelligence, to your consciousness, to the breath, to the center of love, when you sleep? When you are in a state of deep sleep you are not aware of anything. But the moment you are awake, if somebody calls you a name, you get angry; if somebody hurts your child, you get angry. During deep sleep, however, your mind is never angry, because in sleep there is no such content in the mind. Sleep is that state of mind without any sort of content. As long as some content is there, you cannot be asleep; you are either awake or dreaming.

One day I tried to do an experiment. I wondered what happens during that time when sleep comes. I studied my anatomy and physiology—and then for three days I could not sleep, because I was watching the sleep! Insomnia can be cured very easily. It exists because there is something in the mind that does not allow one to take rest and that creates the insomnia. That groove in the mind is so deep that the mind spontaneously goes to that thought pattern, and then a helplessness is there and one cannot sleep or rest.

Many problems and diseases can be cured by deep sleep. Doctors always say that you should have adequate rest. When you are fed up with your children, even though you love them dearly, you say, "Let me rest." The best kind of rest that you have known so far as a human being is called sleep, although it is not really the best rest possible.

When you are tired of the joys of the world—even the best of the joys, as when a woman and man make love—then you are tired because there is a limit to what you can enjoy. Then people want to rest, which means that the joy prolongs itself into the rest. There are two types of rest. One is when you are rested and go to sleep. You know that you were in a state of deep sleep and deep joy because you were not disturbed, you did not dream, your body was relaxed in the morning, and you did not find any signs of fatigue and strain. That is why you know you had a good rest, and slept well: your body and mind tell you that you slept well.

But not all possible rest is provided by sleep. If you watch a person, he may be snoring, but if a fly lands on him or he gets tired of a position, he moves. If he were really in a deep sleep, then he would not be aware of that. This means that a part of the mind still remains awake, even if you are in a state of deep sleep. That part of the mind should be understood; it is that part of the mind that observes you, and knows how much rest you need. When you are completely rested, then that part of the mind decides that you have taken enough rest, and wakes you up.

Some people sleep too much on their left side, and some people sleep too much on the right. After eating food, you should sleep on the left side. You should try to have a balanced sleep. To aid your digestion, you can rest while placing a pillow under the left armpit. There is one problem in this method: if you put a pillow under your side, the circulation is disturbed—so after that specific exercise, change your position. Do not use the pillow and then sleep in that position, or in the morning or in a few days' time you will find that the blood circulation has decreased. This exercise helps the digestion. It helps to open the right nostril, the sun or pingala nadi. After lunch, or after heavy food, or when you want to relax, you should lie on the left side. When you are tired—for example if you are a jogger and you have done vigorous exercise, or if you have some heart problem, or if your arteries are blocked—you should sleep more on the right side and give the heart rest. In these conditions—when you are fatigued or strained—you should learn to lie down on your right side.

You cannot sleep continuously. If you really study sleep you will learn that the human being can never really sleep for more than three hours. Because everyone else is sleeping, there is no one to communicate with, so there is a tradition, an understanding, that you need eight hours of rest. But you really are in dreamless sleep only three hours. If you calculate all the minutes and seconds, you cannot sleep for more than three hours.

Who sleeps? The mind wants to sleep because it needs rest. You should allow it to go to that state of mind where there is no content. The great sages, however, felt that sleep is a waste of time, because you do not know what happens to you during sleep. When sleep comes you become unconscious, you are in a deep, unconscious state, and that gives you rest. And then when you wake up you think that you rested. That is not really good; actually you should learn to rest consciously. You can learn to have conscious sleep.

Meditation is that state in which you give conscious rest to the mind. The difference between sleep and meditation, or sleep and samadhi, is similar to two people going to see a great man—one sleeps there because he is tired, but the other talks with the great man. You are actually very close to the Reality when you sleep, but you are not conscious of it; another person, who is fully conscious and experiences the Reality, is in samadhi. There is really very little difference. The difference between samadhi, sleep, death, and meditation is only a fine line of demarcation. In meditation you do not allow your consciousness to drift.

If we add up the time spent in sleep throughout our lives, we find that we sleep for the equivalent of twenty years. Can you imagine a person being dead for twenty years? Why do we say that death is terrifying, when we do not think that sleep is terrifying? We want to sleep; should we not also want to die? The differences between these two experiences should be understood. Sleep is always used for ignorance; one who is asleep is in a deep state of ignorance. This ignorance is one in which you completely lose awareness of both sides—awareness of eternity, and awareness of the world. You gain only rest; you are merely obtaining sleep so that you can wake up. That is the only benefit sleep provides. Sleep relieves you from all pains; sleep gives you rest and energy, so that you can again cope with situations—but sleep does not make you intelligent; it does not give you knowledge.

So the sages said, "Let us overcome this. Let us meditate." They practiced a state called "sleepless sleep." Samadhi means sleepless sleep in the modern language. The sages found a way of going into that state in which they are sleeping, yet they remain awake. There is a Sanskrit word about this that can be interpreted in many ways. Night is enjoyed by different kinds of people. The night that is used by the ignorant for *bhoga*, for sensual pleasure, the same night is used by yogis for divine pleasure. Sensual pleasure does not last for a long time; divine pleasure leads you toward everlasting bliss.

We know what divine bliss is because we had a drop of sensual pleasure, and we repeated it, wanting that pleasure to last forever, to merge into it. Your partner wants to merge into it, to attain that, but it is not possible. You do not have the capacity to do that. Nobody has ever done it, since sensual pleasure has a limited capacity.

So we ask if there is another way that we can attain that bliss in which there is no pain. If two people repeatedly make experiments in life, doing all these pleasurable things, collecting things, owning things, and enjoying all these pleasures, they will finally decide that this world has no capacity to give them eternal joy or eternal bliss. The day they understand that, they go beyond the three states of waking, dreaming, and sleeping, and then they attain the fourth state, from which they can see all three states separately. They can see themselves sleeping; they can then see themselves dreaming; they can see themselves waking. Yet they are still there. The fourth state is a state of enlightenment.

This particular process of going from waking to dreaming to sleeping, and then going beyond, has two methods or routes; there are two ways there. The first is to expand your consciousness with consciousness. In the waking state, you are using only a small part of the mind. You use that awareness during the waking state.

You do not have control over that part of the mind that is dreaming and sleeping. If you have control over these two parts, then the totality of the mind is under your control. Your mind becomes a powerful instrument, and then you can really use that mind. That is a great mind!

How do we begin this process? The yogis first realized that sleep wastes many hours: it is not necessary that the night be used for sleeping alone. In addition to sensual pleasure or meditation, you can also utilize the night for many creative arts, for studies, poetry, practice, and to converse with somebody whom you love. The idea that eight hours of sleep are needed is a myth accepted by medical science. How does medical science know that eight hours is helpful, and what is supposed to occur after eight hours of sleep? The state hospitals are packed with patients who sleep for eight hours, but that does not help them. Medical science is not exploring other dimensions of healing. They put people into a sleep state by injecting drugs; they use anesthesia for pain and sleeping medications for sleep. But that is not the way to help people.

The sages say, "Come back, come home. There is another way we can function. We have already discovered it. One day you will finally come home, but by that time you may have become completely disoriented and completely disorganized by that modern type of treatment. You have energy now; you are living. Use that life-force to attain the final goal. Do not waste your time! Wake up from the ignorance of sleep." The waking state is definitely higher than the sleep state, but when you wake up, do not dissipate yourself and your energy.

You want to go to that which is beyond, to attain *turiya*, the fourth state. You can attain that state. If you can earn money or do all the things you do in the world, why can you not accomplish something in the inner world? You are never lost inside; you are always lost outside. Do not be afraid to meditate. Be confident that you will not become lost—you are within yourself.

The word "yoga" has been vulgarized and does not mean anything now. We are discussing a particular method that leads you to conscious, deep sleep, and yet you remain awake in that state. That state is very beneficial; it is very close to samadhi. To learn this method you need to have a definite time set aside, so that you can practice at the same time every day. You need to regularly devote this time to these practices. This is a key point. Sometimes students say they will sit and meditate, but after the fourth, fifth, or seventh day they are sleeping or reading the newspaper at that hour. Serious students know that they should determine that no matter what happens, this one time is totally devoted to the Lord of Life, to the process of enlightenment. At that time all other things are secondary.

You are trying to reach and touch that infinite Source which is only One, self-existent. You have the capacity to do that. No human being is weak. He makes himself weak when he becomes the victim of his habit patterns and his senses, and when his mind starts identifying with the objects of the world. To overcome weakness you must be sincere and honest to the Lord of Life. This is paying attention to the Source. You feed your body good food, you feed your mind with good books, but how are you feeding the quest of your soul? How are you quenching your thirst? You cannot deny that Source from which you received this life. Who gave you this life? Who gave life to your ancestors, to the first people on the earth? Who gave you this earth? Who gave you blood? The ultimate Reality, the Source, gave it to you. This is His blood flowing in our veins.

All your breath sings a song eternal—"so-ham, so-ham, so-ham"—but you are not listening to that. Your heart is creating a sound—"lub-dub, lub-dub"—but you are not listening to that, either. Your brain is singing and you do not hear it. You are busy listening to mere sounds that are useless or meaningless, and which have adverse effects on your mind. Learn to put yourself into silence. Your normal habit, your training, and your education is to go to the ocean of the external world and become lost in the sounds. Learn instead to go back to the Source.

Going to the Source of silence is using the method of meditation, the inward journey. But usually your mind becomes a wall, blocking your progress. You need to learn how to focus your mind, because only a small part of mind has been trained. When you use a small part of your mind to try to develop a new discipline, then your whole mind becomes agitated, and that is why you cannot meditate for some time.

A second problem is that you have no patience. Americans are especially and extraordinarily brilliant in the world, because they have confidence that they are financially secure. But there is one bad tendency: they have no patience, because nobody teaches them patience. They sow the seeds today, and tomorrow morning they expect results. When you have done some action, you do not wait for the reaction to occur. You fall asleep before that happens, and during sleep the reaction occurs. The waking state slips into the dreaming and sleeping states. You need to learn to be patient with yourself.

Learning to have self-dialogue and a time for meditation are techniques that will help develop patience. This does not mean that you should be complacent. You should be content, but you should never be satisfied. Contentment is something that should be there all the time. Whatever action you have undertaken, the fruits of your actions should not create discontentment in you. You should create contentment in yourself; if you are discontent you cannot properly perform the next action. To be satisfied means to become lazy and pacified. Do not encourage that part of mind that becomes apathetic all the time.

Childhood and old age are the same. A child is innocent, and though he commits many mistakes, he is forgiven. Old age is full of follies, because the same thought patterns occur over and over. These repetitious thoughts will blast your attempts at meditation. A preoccupied mind is not healthy. That is the reason you need to learn to have a dialogue and talk to your mind, so that you know that your mind is not preoccupied with stupid thoughts. Lack of preparation for meditation is unhealthy.

Just as there are different seasons in the year, so also are there seasons in the mind. Sometimes the mind feels joy, sometimes not. You can also learn to create a joyous state of mind by the technique of applying *sushumna* before you meditate. But first you should understand and accept that whatever you have learned up to this time— and in the future for as long as you live, even if you learn your whole life—is only about the waking state. You will not understand the deeper experiences because there is no training available in the world for that.

The yogis say to expand, not contract, your consciousness during the waking state. When you expand yourself, what will happen? Through expansion of the waking state you can attain *turiya*. Expanding means you are making use of the waking state. You make the waking state a means to expand your consciousness, to widen your little field of mind, which has got many barriers and fences. You are expanding the field of mind.

For expanding the mind, one should understand two

laws of life: one is contraction, and the other is expansion. In expansion one learns to love, serve, and to give selflessly; in contraction one goes on building the boundaries around oneself by becoming selfish, egotistical, and finally miserable. To be on the path of selflessness enhances and enriches the human personality and potentiality. It is just like creating a taste for music. Those who have a taste for classical music are considered to be cultured. In spirituality, expansion of the mind is important—and for that a student should learn to direct mind, action, and experience according to the goal he wants to attain: selfless actions, speech that relates to the factual world, and a mind that learns to fathom the inner dimensions of life. There are also other methods for expanding this state, called "love without object." You do not need some object to love; there is a quality of love that is called love without an object. That quality comes after a long time.

When you expand the field of the mind, the dream state and the sleep states come under the waking state, within its realm. Then you are in turiya. This is not easy. When you learn to expand your mind both horizontally and vertically, you make it a cross. The symbol of the cross is unique and can be interpreted in many ways. A yogic way of interpretation is that there are two main hemispheres in our subtle body: upper and lower. These two hemispheres meet and form a cross at the heart center between the two breasts. Expanding the mind means visualizing the vast width and height mentally. Draw an unending line horizontally and lead your mind to try to reach the limitless ends. Do the same vertically. Make the base of your spine one end and draw the line upwards. It is just like trying to climb the stairs into the infinite sky.

It will become an eternal cross and there will be no end. Yet, you have to learn to go even beyond that. Let your dreaming state become the waking state and your sleeping state also become the waking state, with the help of the technique of *yoga nidra* (see chapter 11), and thus attain *turiya*, the state beyond.

CHAPTER FIVE

Relationships

*K*NOWINGLY OR UNKNOWINGLY, your kundalini has awakened if you are dynamic, if you have attained something in your life that is uncommon, unusual, exceptional. Those are the results of the rise of kundalini. Many students are interested in kundalini, the spiritual energy, but they do not really understand it. We will discuss the power of kundalini in greater detail later, but first you need to understand how to work with your personality in the waking state, because that is where you create obstacles for yourself.

Do not think that you can accomplish the task of becoming enlightened outside the world. Yes, you need time to do practice, but to have that, you need to adjust your time in the world. There are some people who are systematic in their practice, but they are dry and harsh with others. They bother their spouse and children. But there are other people who are loving and adjust their personal lives to attain enlightenment in this lifetime, here and now. You have to have determination.

Partners sometimes become critical of each other's paths. Never think that someone else is not practicing well, and that you are practicing well. That is not spirituality. If you are practicing well you should be happy, not jealous, when somebody else is practicing.

In spirituality there is no jealousy. There may be competition, but not jealousy. Yes, you can compete with your partner. If your partner is very spiritual, then you will also become more spiritual—that is good for you. But to think that your partner is spiritual and to feel bad because you are not as spiritual is not helpful. Never create such negative competition in your life.

There is one important principle—Truth—that you want to use in all your relationships in the external world. Do not speak any truth that is injurious, hurting, or harming—for that is not real truth. According to yoga science it is not truth that should be practiced first, it is love that should be practiced first. And there is a difference between love and truth: truth without love is a vacant, empty experience. No manual in the world really explains what love is, except the teachings of yoga. Yoga says love is *ahimsa*—a means "not," *himsa* means "killing, harming, or injuring."

So, when you try to practice love, you should first practice not hurting, harming, or injuring. Do not go to the external world to practice this; begin with the nearest one whom you love most, and practice this with him or her, because you took vows when you married. When you have accepted somebody as your best friend, to whom you can relate, speak, share, and feel, then first practice not harming, hurting, or injuring them. This is actually love in practice. Resolve that no matter what happens you will never try to injure, harm, or hurt the one you love. Sometimes you mean something but your partner thinks you mean something different. Sometimes your firmness, determination, and your *sankalpa shakti*—resolve or determination—are misunderstood. Never make your partner weak. You often want your partner to lean on you, and you make him or her weak, but that is not healthy. When you love somebody, usually you do not love them intensely, so you do not really enjoy it. No object or person has the capacity to fulfill you. It is the intensity of your love, your sensitivity, that makes you enjoy it. Do not lose that sensitivity.

Life and relationships are very close to each other; they are virtually one and the same. If you are related to somebody, it means that somebody wants something from you, and you want something from them, and you are sharing with each other. That is what a relationship is: a relationship means sharing. Sometimes it is mutual, sometimes it is not—most of the time it is not. When a relationship becomes imbalanced, one-sided, and demanding, then a sickness starts and you want to leave.

But you cannot live without relationships. They are necessary for you to live in the world, no matter in what capacity you serve, whether you are a priest, a renunciate, an ordinary householder, or a man of the world. You have to learn to communicate: life is relationships and communication. Communication is very important, and as we discussed, communication starts from your thoughts, not your behavior.

You have to learn to express yourself in such a way that you become an example, so that you become useful, so that your knowledge is shared and understood, your knowledge is received by others. It becomes part of your education. You have to learn to understand that law of communication in the external world; otherwise you are a failure.

Communication is an essential part of the education that is imparted at home. If the parents do not communicate well with the children, then the children have that problem to the last breath of their life. No one can help them—not psychology, philosophy, or therapy—because in childhood the seeds are sown so deeply.

When you have children, you have to go out of your way to change yourself. You are great teachers, but you also have to learn something from them: learn humor and joy. How do they have that irrepressible joy, so that they jump with joy all the time? They do not care for the things that you consider best, and those things to which you give no value, they value, just as they build a house on the sand. They do not care for your wealth, bank balance, intelligence, or the certificates and degrees that you have received from colleges and universities. They are in joy and they are happy—they are better than you in many ways.

In contrast, watch how attached you are to your family. You call it love, but that is not true. It is not love; it is selfishness and attachment. Whenever you are attached, you are selfish. In love you give; in attachment you take. In attachment you do not want to give; you want to have. There is a vast difference between having and giving. Those who learn to give are called lovers. Those who learn only to receive are beggars. Those who have deep attachments do great injury to others and to themselves. Those who share and give freely do great service to those they love. There is a vast difference between love and attachment.

Usually, you expect too much from the world. There are actually two worlds: the world created by you, and the world created by Providence. What creates problems for you is created by you, by your mother, father, brothers, sisters, and your relationships.

The world created by you creates problems for you. Somehow in the past, you expected the future. Learn to arrange your world so that it does not create problems for you. You are a human being, and you have the power, the understanding, and the knowledge. Instead, you waste your energy calling on God, expecting Him to solve your problems. You repeat the same thing with your wife or husband. You expect something which he or she does not have.

Expectation is the mother of all misery in relationships. If you did not expect so much, you would be happy. Having no expectations means happiness. Share, enjoy, and give freely to each other whatever you have. That should be the formula. Expecting too much from each other brings misery and leads to divorce. You will enjoy love when you do not expect it from others. The moment you expect, then you start calculating, and then you are frustrated—and you go to another man or another woman, and then again you become frustrated.

Neither the East nor the West is completely happy. After counseling many couples in both the East and West, I have learned that no one is happy, because only one who is within is happy. One who is within understands what the concept of real happiness is.

You feel love for each other and "lost" when you meet as a man and woman because the senses contact matter, and as a result of that, you either experience pain or joy. But beyond that joy there is another joy, called mental joy, and beyond that there is spiritual joy. Beyond that still further is a state of absolute joy. Learn to go beyond the physical plane and not become lost or scattered in that experience.

We are all traveling to that source of silence—you can call it God, you can call it Ishvara, you can call it Nirvana or whatever you want. There are many paths—a variety of languages and paths—but they go to one Source. It may be called by different names; we have many names for the sun. You say that you want God, but you may merely be pushing away some realities that you want to forget. You are escaping from something, but you say that you are searching for God. Actually you are searching for a good partner for yourself and you cannot be honest about that, so you say you want God. Be honest with yourself: what do you really want? Ask yourself if your desire is genuine and helpful. If this particular want is fulfilled, will you be happy? No want, even if fulfilled, can make you happy, because that fulfillment only brings another want, and then you again try to fulfill it—throughout your whole life you go on adding fuel to the fire, which creates only smoke, but no fire.

On the path of practice one can be misunderstood. Many marriages fall apart on the path of spirituality. If your partner is not spiritual and does not understand your path, if she or he gets in your way, you can never practice spirituality. It destroys your spirituality. You and your partner should have a complete understanding. Then you can practice. If one of you does not want to make progress, the other cannot.

If you want to live in the world, lead a spiritual life. Without it, life is hell. And to do that, learn to adjust, to understand each other. Then something will be possible. Otherwise, watching the world all alone, living in the world, you will be misunderstood and you will be nagged, you will be pulled back to a lower level, and there will be a downfall. Then your time and energy are wasted. You need to discuss your goals with your partner, to tell them this is a prime condition of your life, it is your hunger and thirst. You want to walk the spiritual path, and you can help each other. A woman can help her husband. There has actually been a great woman behind every great man of the world. Women are a great power. Women can enlighten themselves, and they can also help others. The power that women have, men do not have—but that which a man has, a woman also needs. So you can organize your lives well if you understand and cooperate that way.

If you are alone, then that is also well and good. Do not use someone else as a crutch. The great Being is seated within you; why do you not converse with it? In this poisonous tree of life, one of the beautiful fruits is *satsanga*. Satsanga means to be aware of *satya*, truth, all the time. If the Lord of Life cannot protect you, how can you be protected by a little man whose body is frail and subject to change, death, and decay? If you are not safe with the Lord of Life, how can you be safe in anyone's hands? If you do not accept the Lord of Life as your Reality and savior, your master and guide, how can any man or woman help? With such ideas you can strengthen yourself within.

Do not create conflicts for your partner. Do not push your partner to do practice; you should give each other mental freedom. There is a lot of difference between the East and the West. In the East you are mentally free. You live in one home, and every child is mentally free to worship or accept spirituality the way they wish. Spirituality is a must in their life, but each can go on any path of spirituality.

In the West it is not like that; it is very rigid. In the West there is mental bondage. But in the East there is physical bondage: you cannot marry anybody you want or bring somebody home and disturb the whole family. There is a social bondage in the East, and in the West is mental bondage. Thus both East and West are suffering.

There are many points that clearly define the difference between East and West. But all human beings are human beings. All human beings have one and the same idea as far as spirituality is concerned. Your adjustment should lead to contentment—and if you are content in life, you are happy. Happiness is completely in your hands, and not in the hands of God.

God will not make you happy. God is already in you! God is everywhere. Why do you look to external circumstances for happiness? You lean on others. Every woman dreams of getting married to somebody who will make her happy, but that is not possible. No man can make a woman happy, and no woman has the capacity to make a man happy. They both want happiness from each other. Then happiness disappears, and expectations grow and grow, and then they both become discontented.

Happiness exists the moment you learn that the great person for whom you were searching is within you. This little tiny man or woman outside is just a sort of external companion with whom you can be happy. The day a woman learns to adore her husband because he is her husband, and a means for her in the external world, but he is not her Lord of Life, then she will understand happiness. The same is true for a man.

The problem is that you expect something great and powerful from something small and limited. You get irritated and tell each other, "You don't make me happy"—but no one can make you happy. You are right, and he is right, but you are both unhappy because of your bad concepts.

Do not expect happiness from anyone; that is something that you can find only within. Happiness and unhappiness are concepts you form in the mind. When you become selfish, you want something your own way. If you do not get that in your own way, you get angry, and that is called unhappiness. Try to understand reality; if you see things as they are, you will never be unhappy. If you accept things as they are, you will never be unhappy. Then, you do not expect too much from reality. The world of objects is subject to change, death, decay, and decomposition. You need to see the world as it is, to face the reality that one day you will leave this platform.

You were born here because you wanted to be an American living in America. That was your choice. Your birth was not God's choice, it was your choice. You have the willpower to come or to go; to do or not to do; to be happy or to be unhappy. God is not responsible for this; He loves you all equally. The law of love that flows freely and equally, without any obstruction, from eternity to eternity, is called the Lord of Life. You are unhappy because you do not understand that law. You do not want to be responsible—but if you are not responsible, nothing happens.

Develop inner strength. External strength does not help you; that which helps you is inner strength. Gentleness is the greatest of all strengths. Gentleness means that love is expressed with mind, action, and speech. When your mind is one-pointed your actions do not become distorted—and when your speech also follows, there is only love. Then peace comes, because love brings peace. Love does not bring lust. Lust is limited to the senses. Love goes down deep to the soul level, where you understand that you are a ripple of bliss, and your partner is also a ripple of bliss. Then you ask yourself how you can hurt this other ripple, because you are actually two children of eternity. The wife knows her husband is a child of eternity, and the husband understands his wife is a child of eternity.

If you begin your love from there, there is no conflict, no separation, and no disturbance. But you start your relationships through the body. You think that when you got married your wife was slim, but today she has become overweight. You start seeing all the bad things in each other. Your love should grow from the senses to the mind, and from mind to spirit—that is true love. If love does not grow, it is not love. There is only one thing that grows in the universe, and that is love.

Love has been traveling for eternity. The human being also is traveling on the path of this journey, and his love travels to that final goal. Then the call of the senses does not affect him. If you have really examined the body, and its needs, wants, and desires, then you see only one Reality. When you learn to lovingly, skillfully, and selflessly manage your relationships, then you awaken the fires of light and love within. This is what we came here to accomplish.

CHAPTER SIX

First Steps Toward Self-Transformation

*Y*OU HAVE THE CAPACITY and strength to expand your conscious mind with the help of a method that is called "interior research," the internal journey. When a door is locked, if you have the key you can go to the door, find the hole, put in the key, and open the door. This instruction is leading you on the path called "the path of the keyless door." Usually the door is locked and there is no key, but you are learning to open it. You have to open it, and you have the power to do so. You have to be a master if you really want to enjoy life here—the master of your mind. Your mind is yours; know your mind. To open the door and start your inner journey you need to learn several points and to apply them systematically. The following self-transformation program, including *yoga nidra* practice, will definitely help you if you follow it conscientiously and systematically. While sleep cannot really help you, and death cannot transform you, *yoga nidra* (yogic sleep) and this program can help you.

Now, you must pay careful attention. Sometimes teachers do not go very far in their instruction because they see that you are not really paying attention. If you want to be successful in your life, learn to train your attention. Attention is the key point that leads you to concentration, then to meditation, and then to samadhi. But basically this process begins with attention. To attend to one thing at a time and not to allow any intruding thoughts is a skill one should learn. Teach your children that when they eat their food it should be with full attention; when they play they should play. When they talk to you they should give you full attention, and you should also give them full attention.

You actually project and create fears for your children, because you do not pay attention to them: you are talking to someone else and you are casually talking to them, and they learn these bad habits from you. Pay attention to your children even if they are joking with you; you should talk to them with full attention. This is very important. If you could not or did not do something in your life, you see that your children do those things, and then your desires are fulfilled through them. When many of your desires in life are not fulfilled, then you have children and they fulfill your desires. So then you are freed from those desires and fulfilled.

Along with the development of attention, a second quality is the ability to make mistakes without condemning yourself. Determine that no matter what happens, no matter how many times you stumble, it does not matter. If you have not crawled, you cannot walk; if you have not stumbled, you cannot stand. In the process of unfoldment you have to crawl, and without crawling you will have psychological problems. So do not be afraid of stumbling. You will stumble many times in life. You will commit many mistakes. Don't create a complex in your heart and mind by thinking that you are nothing. Don't start condemning yourself, and suffering. Stumbling and committing mistakes are not sins. On the path of wisdom there is no such thing as sin. This does not mean that a person can commit a crime and say it is not wrong. What you call a "sin" is a state that leaves an imprint on your mind, a negative imprint that settles in your unconscious mind. You can be free by understanding this.

"Sin" is an undefined word that hounds your mind and life and creates a barrier for you. All the world's religions—whether Hinduism, Islam, Judaism, or Christianity—talk about sin, but none of them really explains it. A sin is any act that affects your mind in a negative way. Then, if you remain in a state of negativity for some time, you become passive and helpless. A passive mind is very dangerous. A negative mind can be improved, but a passive mind leads to sickness; it can make even a doctor sick. For example, if a healthy doctor is hired to work in an asylum, he may also become crazy after some time, if he does not have the strength to take the negative situation. He may identify himself with the patients and thus become crazy.

Never identify yourself with negativity, with a passive mood, or with weakness. You are not that. You have many weaknesses, yet you, yourself, are not weak. You commit many mistakes, yet you are not weak. You have committed many so-called sins, yet you are not a sinner. If you think that you have sinned, then how can confessing it to another human being like yourself help you?

When you observe what your problems are, don't become disappointed and start condemning yourself. At that point decide that you will help yourself—but do not take on too big a project. You often fail because you try to do too much. For interior research you need to begin with a small project.

One problem is that your principles are different from your practice. Your actual practice is different from what you know and believe. When you commit mistakes, the real repentance is in not repeating them. If you are helpless, practice. If you stumble, practice again. Help will come to you; grace will be there. Do not give up with your human endeavors! Whether you consciously or unconsciously commit a mistake, just do not do it again, but do not believe in sin.

Every action creates a reaction. When you remember the Lord you gain mercy, blessings, and grace. This is an automatic reaction, like hitting a ball against a wall so that it comes back to you. The result depends on how you strike the ball, your intensity, and your aim. Your aim, intensity, feeling, and zeal are important: you need to have zeal for practice. Usually, however, you care only for trivial or mundane things of the external world. Your eyes flow with tears for petty things, but your heart should cry for something higher. If you constantly cry for worldly things, your body will become ill—but if you cry for God, you will move toward samadhi, ecstasy. At present, you have great zeal to attain worldly things—you have too much feeling for the things of the world.

Your main problem is that you are hung up on the things of the world: you are afraid you will not gain what you want, and you are always afraid of losing what you have. You have never worked with the totality of your mind. This anxiety is all the result of your mind—because nothing happens to the body, and nothing happens to God: whatever happens, it occurs only in your mind. The Upanishads say that atman is the fastest entity—and yet, at the same time, it has no movement. Teachers often say that the mind is the fastest, faster even than sound or light. But there is one thing faster than the mind: your individual soul, the atman. It is the fastest because wherever the mind travels, the soul is already there, no matter where the mind goes. So if there is anything that can correct and help your mind, it is not worldly wealth or objects, it is nothing external, but only that which is the innermost center of your being.

Do not concern yourself with the rewards of meditation. There is a scientific law that every action has a reaction; it is not possible for an action to not have benefits. Even if you do not see conscious benefits, there are unconscious results. At the very least you will develop muscle relaxation, rid yourself of tension and stress, and learn to use the mind for spirituality.

The Program

First we will describe the program's important steps in order, and then describe each point comprehensively and in full detail.

Step One. Practice sitting in meditation at the same time every day to create additional patterns, new grooves or habits in the mind.

Step Two. Learn to have an internal dialogue with yourself within your mind.

Step Three. Develop a still, steady, yet comfortable posture for meditation.

Step Four. Develop a pattern of serene breath.

Step Five. Cultivate *sankalpa*, or determination; that is, establish your willpower. Before you do something, you have to determine that you will do it, that you have to do it, and that you can do it. That is determination.

Step Six. Learn to let go of any distracting thought that comes into your mind. It should not remain there. You should not brood on any particular thought, no matter how wonderful or how bad it is.

Step Seven. Introspection. Inspect your thoughts; see which thoughts are worthwhile to cultivate. The yoga manuals talk about two types of thoughts: *klishta* and *aklishta.* The first is helpful; the latter is harmful, injurious. Helpful thoughts are those that inspire you or encourage your effort. Injurious thoughts involve thinking, for example, that you are good for nothing, or inferior. These are negative thoughts. You need to inspect your thoughts to determine which help you, and which should be eliminated.

Step Eight. Witnessing. When you have learned to witness the things of the world—when you are not identifying with the things of the world—then you have become a seer.

Step One: The Importance of a Regular Practice Time

You should practice and do your meditation at the same time every day. Regularity in time is very important. A habit is a pattern that is formed. If you repeat the same thing again and again, in time it becomes a part of your personality. It becomes a deep habit. After death, you go neither to hell nor heaven, but remain in your unconscious habit patterns. The whole of the theory, philosophy, and psychology of the yoga practices is used to change habit patterns. That changes your character and personality. Habit patterns compose the fabric that is called personality. So you can either cultivate good habits and strengthen your personality, or allow your mind to stay with its negative patterns. Meditation should become a regular habit. But it should not be done as mere ritual. Mere rituals do not become a real part of life, because you do not do them with a full heart. Do your meditation every day at exactly the same time, no matter what happens. Make it prominent in your life. Some days you will stumble, some days you will do it—but finally, if you are persistent, you will have time.

Students should examine their priorities and ask themselves what is prominent in their lives. Is your enlightenment most important, or is it food or sex? You need to decide on one, because you have not decided on that so far. Once you have decided, then you will have to find the way of doing this. What you do with your decision is important; otherwise, although people decide, they cannot carry out the practice.

You should have an understanding with your spouse and children. Arrange your time in such a way that no matter what happens, that time is not given to anything but your practice. This time for practice should not be a time in which you are rushed or in haste. Discuss your goals with your partner so that she or he does not misunderstand you. A mutual understanding between partners should be there, so that there is no disturbance. Sit in a quiet corner, sit under a tree, sit in a garden, or sit near a pool. You are blessed with all the means in life, but you are not blessed by yourself. Let yourself have the blessings from within.

Just as you have set times for your essential duties, so also should you set a time for meditating. This is the key point in your progress. Determine that no matter what happens—life or death—you will sit down to meditate. Sometimes your mind does not want to meditate. Tell yourself that it does not matter: you have to do your duty—and sit down. Many times the mind goes through fluctuations and roams around—but just sit down and just do the practice. If you do not want to meditate, then do not meditate. You should not fight with your mind; you should have a gentle dialogue with your mind. You will learn many things when you enter into this kind of self-dialogue.

Step Two: Developing an Internal Dialogue

The next step is a very important one, but one that few students understand. To succeed in meditation you have to develop this important step. You do not begin with meditation itself. First you learn to set a regular meditation time, and then to have a dialogue with yourself. In this process you are coming in contact with your inner, internal states. You are learning about the subtle aspects of your mind, your own conscience—and at the same time you are also training yourself. If you don't have time to have a dialogue with yourself, to fulfill the purpose of your life, that is a sin. The greatest of all sins in life is to kill your own internal conscience, the teacher within. You are constantly killing yourself, your atman, your conscience. You know that self-training is right, and yet you are not doing it. If you make a mistake, have a dialogue with yourself. If you have a dialogue with yourself for a few minutes or hours before you do meditation, then your meditation will be good. If you do not do that, then you use your meditation time for self-dialogue, and then the "meditation" is not really meditation.

So before you begin to try to meditate, you should sit down and talk to yourself, have a dialogue. In this manner many problems can be solved, and you will receive new insights. The state of meditation may not yet have actually been developed, but you can just relax and have a dialogue with yourself at exactly the same time. This kind of dialogue should not be related to the things you have done, your office, or your family.

Your task is to cultivate a relationship with your own mind—a relationship in which questions about the purpose of life can be fruitfully raised. Ask the mind to deal with major questions like the purpose of life. Ask the mind why it disturbs you when you want to meditate. Then you will see how the mind reacts to you. The mind has many aspects: sometimes the mind becomes like a child—it wants you to nourish that naughty child. When the mind becomes a magician, that is very disturbing: it plays tricks all the time! To talk to your mind you will have to accept one of the relationships with your mind. Do you want to teach your mind as a brother, as a father, or as a mother? You have to decide which aspect or relationship you want to have with your mind. If I want to have a dialogue with my mind, then am I a servant of my mind, a secretary, or a friend?

This process of dialogue is very important. You will enjoy it, provided you take the time to do it well. In each twenty-four-hour period you have time to sleep, to dream, to eat, and to do other things—but you think that you cannot talk to yourself. Learn to make some time for this. If you like, go somewhere quiet, park your car, and just start talking to yourself. Have a good, pleasant dialogue.

When you begin to have a dialogue with the mind, you will notice that you are not honest with yourself— and you are never honest with other people either, no matter how much you claim to be, because you are not honest with yourself. At least once a day, for a few minutes, you should be honest with yourself.

One of the rules of psychotherapy about the contract between a therapist and a patient is that both parties have to be honest. Sometimes the therapist has to say something that he does not want to say, but the contract is that both will be honest in expressing themselves.

In self-therapy the situation is somewhat different: you have to talk to your mind honestly, not by thinking of it as your boss, but as your finest instrument. To talk to your mind, you should have confidence. You have to realize that the mind is yours, but it has taken over.

You can accept yourself, no matter who you are. You can be accepted by yourself, provided you learn how to forgive yourself. People do not forgive themselves, and that is why they condemn themselves. Learning to forgive yourself means to decide that if you have done something against your wish, will, or desire, you will recognize it as a mistake but decide to forgive yourself.

So in this process you start a dialogue, talking to yourself and asking what your purpose is. You should consider that your mind is yours. It is not some foreign element, either something great, devilish, or strange: if you think that, then you cannot have a real dialogue; and if you do not have a dialogue, you cannot benefit. The first point in the dialogue is to explain to your mind that it is too worldly and materialistic. You tell the mind that it has become dissipated, and it should learn to tread the path of light, love, and devotion. Whatever you say, then follow that decision—become an *apta*. An apta, or a great man, is he who does exactly what he says.

Many experiments have been conducted by the great sages using prayer, meditation, contemplation, ritual, action, and many other techniques. They found that there is only one important resource: the Center of Consciousness, from where consciousness flows on various degrees and grades. Mind alone is nothing.

Examine the mind and how corrupt it is. Mind wants to create distractions, even when a method has been established. For example, if a Christian nun meditates on Christ, sometimes she may meditate on Christ on the cross, then on the Christ Child on Mother Mary's lap, or sometimes on the Christ on the Mount. This is a corruption of the mind, because the mind does not want to accept only one point of concentration. The mind wants variety. Mind is just like the palate, which wants new dishes and foods every day. The mind also does that: it is the mind that taught these senses to have many tastes and cravings. But all the various tastes come from the source called the soul—that spirit, that source of consciousness, from where intelligence, brilliance, and wisdom flow.

When you have established this perspective between yourself and your mind, then you can coordinate the way you think, the way you speak, and the way you act. That is perfect communication. Such a person has the capacity to become a sage. He is an *apta mahapurusha*, a great man. Even avatars bow before such great people, because they are *apta:* they have attained a state of tranquility and equilibrium. Your actions, your speech, and your mind should be well-coordinated.

Your problem is that this inner perspective—and thus your knowledge—is not retained. It is as if you are pouring milk into a bowl with a hole. Your first effort should be to patch that hole, so that when knowledge comes, it is retained. When you expand the capacity you have, you receive knowledge. In the self-dialogue you do not, out of egotism, start controlling your mind—you should start by being a friend. To have a friend is great. Many great devotees establish a relationship with God as a friend. You share what you have with a friend, and he shares what he has—you do not think that you are rich and your friend is poor. To establish a friendship with the Lord you have to be an equal, or else it is a bad friendship, and it will turn into begging.

Understand that your mind is your friend; do not order it around. It will not take anyone's dictation. But also do not allow your mind to order you around. Establish a friendship with your mind. Be a close friend to your mind, a very close friend. Let the mind whisper inner secrets to you, and put all things in front of your mind. This is the contract between you and your great friend, the mind.

Put in front of your mind all your external problems, and your mind will share all its inner secrets and whispers. To do this, you need courage. This path of fire and light is trodden upon only by the person who has courage. If you have your own grace, then you also have the grace of the Lord of Life. If you do not have your personal grace, you do not have the grace of the Lord either. There is a remedy within you—there is a way to help yourself to solve external problems with the inner wisdom you have been given. First, you must learn the art of having an internal dialogue. You should learn to listen to yourself.

Perhaps your mind will tell you there is something beautiful on somebody's table, something you do not have. It may suggest that you quietly pick it up, put it in your pocket, and leave. If so, then you say to your mind, "You have done such things before and regretted it." This dialogue continues—and then your power of determination or will and that inner, latent wisdom that you have says, "All right, mind, go steal—but I will not move my hand to help. Let us see what you can do alone. I am not going to be persuaded. I am determined."

After a few days of such dialogues, your mind will not put such negative suggestions before you again. This is the first step toward victory. Then the mind will never put those thoughts, inclinations, or desires in front of you, knowing that you have trained your senses. This is *tapas*, which means training the senses. Even if you wish to do something wrong, you do not do it. You may be feeling bad or attracted to something, but you do not do it, because you have trained your senses. You have asked your senses not to do something, and they are under your control. That is why in the system of yoga we stress the training of the senses.

If you are a therapist, teacher, or doctor, you can apply this with your patients. You have to inspire them, and help them see the benefits that will come in the future and understand that this will be helpful. Help your patients see that internal wealth and wisdom are coming for them in the future. This helps people get out of the mental grooves of sadness.

The best therapists do not make their patients cry: they give strength. They share their strength with their patients. The best therapists help their patients understand that they have forgotten the best part of themselves, and have come in touch only with their negativity. They help their patients see that there is no limit to their negativity, and that they do not know the best part of themselves.

Each of you has good qualities, but you do not come

in touch with them. You are full of excuses. When you experience your negativity, then you develop many sicknesses. That is why having a dialogue is very important.

When you have a dialogue, your mind has a tremendous capacity, a vast capacity! Your mind can tell you many things—but do not allow your untrained, unpolished, uncontrolled, and uneducated mind to become your teacher: if it becomes your teacher, you are doomed! Let your mind remain a friend. When you talk to a friend it is a question of what you accept and what you do not accept. Do experiments with yourself: how many times does your mind lie, and how many times is it accurate? Establish a friendship with your mind on an equal basis, and do not listen to the mind's temptations. Listen to its suggestions, good ideas, and advice, and learn to observe what type of mind you have.

There are four categories of mind. The first is a completely distorted, distracted, dissipated, and desperate mind, which is not fit for anything. It needs treatment for a long time. The second category or type of mind is that mind that sometimes concludes, "Yes, it is right that I should do something"—but it does not have the strength to follow through, so in a few minutes' time the mind goes back to its negative grooves.

The third type of mind has tasted something; it now wants to attain that, and makes serious efforts to do so. Sometimes it is successful, and sometimes it is not. The fourth type of mind is the mind that knows no other goal or purpose but to penetrate into the deeper folds of life. The student should cultivate this type of mind, which requires training. It is possible for a patient with a totally disorganized mind to develop that one-pointed quality of mind and then attain samadhi.

In India people become swamis or yogis when they are disappointed in life. During that disappointment or crisis they become completely disorganized, and what helps them is the philosophy of nonattachment, *vairagya*. When there is no help at all in the world, and you lose the best of what you have, either you commit suicide—which is not a good thing, but an act of cowardice—or you seek help from the philosophy of nonattachment.

When you have a self-dialogue you may realize that God has graced you with everything. Your wife is good, your children are good, your parents are good, you have everything. So who creates problems for you if you are not at peace? Your mind. You can have a dialogue with the mind and tell the mind, "When you do this to me, you are perhaps the greatest sufferer. You suffer and make the body suffer. Please be my friend."

You need to make the mind your friend—because it is either a great friend, or a great foe. This is true in your daily life as well—your enemy can become a great friend if you know how to make that happen. If you use all your internal resources you will not have an enemy, but you will have a friend; that which is an enemy can be converted into a great friend. In your daily life use the law of *ahimsa*, the law of love. Learn to love; begin by being gentle in your dialogue with yourself.

The process of learning to have an internal dialogue will definitely help you to learn to make a friend of your mind, and then you can begin the process of self-transformation.

CHAPTER SEVEN

Preparing Body and Breath

Step Three: Establishing a Steady Posture for Meditation

Once you have established a regular time for meditation and have learned to have an internal dialogue with yourself, the third step is to develop a steady and comfortable posture. At first you may be very steady but uncomfortable due to a lack of practice. Learn to sit comfortably with a steady and aligned posture.

Steadiness means keeping your head, neck, and trunk in a straight line. You need to keep your spinal column straight because when the head, neck, trunk, and spine are not aligned, then you have a tendency to move in one direction or another. That causes muscle strain, disturbs the mind, and prevents concentration. If the spine is not aligned, then *sushumna*, the central channel, is not aligned and you cannot meditate.

On the spinal column lie three cords: the centralis canalis and the two ganglionated cords of the autonomic system. Energy flows along these cords, which connect the medulla oblongata, the brain, and the balance of the nervous system. If you bend your spinal column you create resistance and do not allow the energy to flow properly. To meditate, you have to see that the four extremities or limbs are arranged in such a way that they do not destroy, distort, or disturb the alignment of the head and spine from the perineum to the medulla oblongata. You should use only one sitting posture, and it should not be distorted. Decide in which posture you are most comfortable. If you are not comfortable sitting on the floor, you can sit on a chair in the friendship pose, which is a very good posture. Your chair or seat should be wooden, because that isolates you from the sensations and subtle vibrations of the earth. Once you understand something about magnetism, static force, and science, then you will come to know that your body is exposed to various types of external energy, so you should sit on something that is a bad conductor of energy. For example, you can use blankets. In the beginning it is better to first place down a wooden plank, and then put blankets on top of that, because they are both bad conductors of heat or energy. Then your energy does not flow outward in any direction; it is intact. You are also not affected by the static energy that is found here, there, and everywhere.

Although you can sit on a chair, those who want to accomplish samadhi, to sit for a long time, to lead a monastic renunciate's life, or to really make meditation part of their life should learn to sit on the floor. If you continue to sit on a chair indefinitely you will sometimes move, which is not good. Your posture should be steady and comfortable. Steadiness of posture means keeping the head, neck, and trunk straight. Even when you walk, learn to walk straight, talk straight, sit straight, and to do everything keeping your head, neck, and trunk straight, so that the spinal column and head are aligned.

Place your hands on your knees. When you sit, form the finger lock by joining the thumb and index fingers, so that there is a circuit of energy. Gently close your eyes and ask your mind to withdraw itself, or create a situation so that the sounds in your home do not disturb you. Meditate at a time when you are not disturbing your spouse and children, when you are not rushing or thinking of other things, and when there is no pressing urgency. Arrange a suitable time when no one can disturb you. During that part of the night that puts everyone into a state of deep sleep, those who are disciplined and want to attain something in meditation remain awake.

You should not try to sit in the lotus pose. Few people in the world can do the lotus pose properly, and to do the lotus pose improperly is unhealthy. You should, however, be inspired by the lotus—it is a symbol that grows in the water and yet remains above the water. So should a yogi live.

Advanced students should use only one posture: the accomplished pose, *siddhasana*, in which you put your left heel at the perineum and the right foot between the leg and thigh, and remain alert. Those who accomplish samadhi do not use any other posture. Sometimes it takes many years to develop a good sitting posture. For beginners, another posture can be used, called *sukhasana*, or the easy pose, a simple cross-legged sitting posture.

In meditation you simply allow your eyes to be gently closed and to rest; you do not roll your eyes or focus on the forehead. There is an external gaze, called *trataka*, that is a good exercise to make your eyes strong—but in meditation, do not focus the gaze or create tension.

Sometimes you sit for a long time, although your

capacity to sit straight is for only a few minutes. Then your spinal cord slowly contracts, which creates a strain and a bend in the spinal column. If you lie down in the crocodile pose and relax there will be no pain. Learn to put yourself in a position so there will be no strain or pain. If you overstretch, there will be pain. If you try to sustain an unbalanced position for some time then you create a hump in the spine, and it is a great punishment for you. You need to learn to align the spine correctly.

You need to establish a steady and comfortable posture in order to achieve a real state of meditation. Work systematically to develop a steady, comfortable, aligned posture.

Step Four: Establishing Serene Breath

After you learn to sit in a comfortable posture, the next step is learning to establish even, deep, diaphragmatic breathing. You need to learn to lead the mind to that fountain that is a fountain of power; there the mind experiences that latent force. You do this with the help of breathing. The twin laws of life involve mind and breath—if you deal with one, you have to deal with the other. By understanding your mind and making it one-pointed, you will learn about breathing—and by learning about your breathing, you will begin to understand your mind.

Presently it is as if you have an immense wealth buried in your own home, but you think you are starving. To awaken that latent power you have to blow away the ashes that have made the fire dormant. To do that, you use a process and a method called even diaphragmatic breathing. That is how you begin to regulate the breath.

In diaphragmatic breathing your abdomen contracts as you exhale. This helps your lungs to expel carbon dioxide. When you inhale you let the abdomen expand, filling the lungs with fresh oxygen. At first you start to regulate the breath by exhaling to a count of eight and then inhaling to a count of eight, or whatever your capacity is.

When your breath is even, the intake and output of your lungs is regulated. When it is regulated, the motions of the lungs themselves are regulated. The heart pumps well, the brain functions well, the nervous system is coordinated, the body is still, and both sets of muscles—the voluntary and involuntary systems—are relaxed. Everything functions correctly. The best way to establish even breathing is to concentrate on the navel center. Exhale to the navel, and then inhale to your comfortable capacity. Then repeat that process. This will regulate your breath. An alternative is to exhale to your toes and come back to the crown of your head. This will help you to make your breath even without counting—because when you count, it sometimes leads you to create a jerk or an irregularity in the breath with each digit.

Diseases give you pain and misery; they take the body to a state of decay. But you can control that by systematically learning how to organize your body, breath, and mind. They are closely related and work together; there is coordination between these parts.

The next step after even breathing is two-to-one breathing. When you are jogging or walking, learn to breathe in a manner in which you inhale to a count of eight and exhale to a count of sixteen. If you do that, you will not become tired for a long time. If you usually can walk for only ten miles, using this exercise you can walk twenty or thirty miles without any tiredness. In this exercise you do not allow the carbon dioxide waste gases to remain inside to create toxins in your body. The bowels, kidneys, lungs, and pores are the four main apertures that clean the body. If your bowels, pores, lungs, and kidneys are efficient, then toxins will not build up in the body. If the body is free of toxins, then it is healthy. Poor food, improper breathing, and even an unbalanced mind can create toxins.

You also create poisons in your body if you are eating food and fighting all the time. You can eat the best food, but it will poison your system if you are upset. Your mind has the power to react to something that is not in the food itself and to create something unhealthy in the food. For example, you can even create blisters in your mouth if you think that the food is contaminated or that it has been touched by somebody you do not like, although there is nothing actually wrong with the food. The mind creates many of our diseases, such as peptic ulcers and other various diseases—in fact, some say seventy percent of the diseases are related to the mind. So learn to be calm, quiet, and at peace when you are doing something. When you want to have sex, to eat, or to sleep, it is important for you to create a harmonious atmosphere. The rest of the time your home can be a circus, but if you have to live together—and want to remain healthy—then at these three times especially you should avoid fighting.

Sometimes fighting is actually therapeutic because you let out your emotions. You express the emotion and let out your anger. If the other person understands you, he can be quiet and allow you to express yourself. Later on, you may apologize for speaking like that. If there is the correct understanding of this, sometimes even swearing and anger are therapeutic agents in human life. However, they should not be used as a habit or as ways of damning or hurting others.

When you have established even breathing, let your

mind watch the flow of the breath. If your mind runs here and there without coordination, there will be a jerk in the breath. Record and observe the breath's behavior; the breath is a barometer of whatever comes into the mind. The study of the breath is a very interesting process: the breath behaves exactly the way the mind behaves, and the mind also behaves exactly the way the breath behaves.

Let your mind flow with the breath. Watch what happens and from where you are breathing. Ask your mind to travel. This breath awareness is also very helpful for the breath, body, and mind. As we said, breath is a barometer of your mind and body. If there is something depressing your mind, the breath will become shallow; if something shocking happens, the breath will have a pause or a gasp—the breath pattern always follows the mind's emotions. With the help of breath awareness, mental control is made possible.

Breath is also the finest focal point for a meditator. When you watch your breath, make sure that there is no noise. Noise means that there is a blockage in the nostrils or that you have a sinus problem; it is not good. The breath should be exhaled and inhaled in such a way that you make it fine, full, and sensitive.

When you are aware of your breath, you become aware of four things: noise, jerks, irregularities, and pauses. The first thing you notice is noise, then jerks or irregularities. When your breath is jerky, the motion of the lungs is related to your heart. If you do diaphragmatic breathing you will notice a difference in your heart rate. If you breathe irregularly with unsystematic changes in length of exhalation and inhalation, it will create another disturbance. Your breath rhythm affects the pumping station of the heart, the blood circulation, the right vagus nerve, the entire digestive system, the liver, and all the other systems. So you should learn to compose yourself and your breath.

The next serious problem to be aware of, which is hard to conquer, is the existence of pauses. You are inhaling and exhaling, but between the inhalation and exhalation you unconsciously create a pause. This should not be done. This kind of pause is a killer; many heart diseases are related to it. You should try to omit that pause mentally. If you are successful, then the inhalation and exhalation will take place without any break. Medical researchers do not teach their patients this about breathing. Experiments are conducted with the mind or the body, but no research has been done with the prana and breath. That kind of research is important, and it should be carried out.

So, first you try to eliminate the pauses in the breath. *Pranayama* means "control of energy"—*prana* means "energy," and *yama* means "control." When you are able to control the pause, the source of many diseases, you have accomplished something. *Puraka* (inhalation) and *rechaka* (exhalation) are not very important, but *kumbhaka* (retention) is very important. Initially, you try to eliminate all pauses. Later, when you intentionally retain the breath, you try to control the length of the pause. In more advanced levels you actually want to learn to increase the pause. Practices involving breath retention should not be undertaken without direct guidance of a qualified teacher—these are more advanced levels wherein one tries to create a long pause consciously; it is another practice entirely.

This conscious pause, created by one who has control over the pause, is a victory over death. The yogis have such control; they control the pauses in their breath. This is part of the secret they have, of not allowing their bodies to fall into the clutches of so-called death. They become free of pain using exercises like *plavini kumbhaka*. If their physical pain is intolerable, they go into a state of *moksha* and are free from pain. Yogis can experience a state of pain, yet be insensitive to it. They can ask a doctor how long an operation will take, and for the duration of that time they can be free of pain. They can control the blood flow and there will be no bleeding. The doctor does not even need to do any suturing. There are actually methods to accomplish that.

The real practice of pranayama starts when you learn how to control the pause, and intentionally develop *kumbhaka*, or retention. Our tradition does not teach kumbhaka to everyone because students must first have a complete knowledge of the *bandhas*, or locks. Second, breath retention by an improperly prepared student may lead to serious physical and mental disorders. You have not prepared yourself because you do not make the time for your practices. To advance in yoga you have to get involved, you have to commit yourself, and you have to do it—then you attain something.

At this point the mind is still not trying to meditate. First we want to practice a technique called "sushumna awakening." Usually one of your nostrils is more active than the other; this is a normal condition. In applying sushumna, you want to allow both nostrils to flow evenly. This has been examined in many universities and research institutes, such as at Yale and Harvard Universities in your country, and at Calcutta and Bombay Universities in India, as well as at centers in Czechoslovakia, Germany, and Russia.

The electric potentials of your right breath are different from your left breath. The electric potentials of your right breath generate heat, while the left breath cools the body. There is a difference in breathing through the right and left nostrils. When you have to do something active, learn to open your right nostril. When you have to do something passive or reflective, allow your left nostril to flow. This process should be under your conscious control. Breathing itself is not under your control, but changing the breath flow is under your control.

The first step in sushumna application is learning to change the flow of the breath with your mental ability, according to your wish and desire. Usually you cannot change it because you do not have control over these two parts of the breath. You should learn to change the flow of the breath, and in this way you can observe the tendency of your mind. There are many mechanical methods described in books by which you can do this, but they are not actually helpful. For example, if you lie down on your left side, the right nostril will become active; if you lie down on the right side, then the left nostril will become active. If you press under your armpit, the opposite nostril will become active. There are many such methods, but they are not really recommended.

To really accomplish this process, you must learn to create a relaxed focus on the right or left nostril. If the nostril is blocked, but not due to some condition like sinusitis, then when the mind focuses on it, that nostril will become active because of the focus of the mind.

If you want to create a situation for meditation you have to pay attention to the point where the nostrils bridge to the upper lip—the point at which your mind notices which nostril is blocked and which nostril is open.

Usually you will notice that one of the nostrils is passive and the other is active. When you have learned to change the flow of the nostrils with your mind, then after some time both nostrils begin flowing evenly. This may take some months or perhaps a year, depending on your capacity and the burning desire within you.

When both nostrils flow evenly the mind cannot worry, because it is disconnected from the senses. Mind does not know how to worry then. It attains a state of joy called *sukhamana*, the joyous mind. That state of mind is conducive to deep meditation. This is an accurate and effective procedure for you to follow, and it is important not to rush or be impatient.

For meditation, the finest of all breathing exercises is sushumna application. When you learn how to apply sushumna, there is no way for your mind to go anywhere but into the inner journey. At present, when you try to meditate you are disturbed and your mind is disturbed. Some days you have a good meditation and other days you do not, depending on your ability in sushumna application.

According to the ancient yoga manuals and the science of yoga, there are three important points in the inward journey. The cream of yoga science is to learn first to apply sushumna; next to awaken kundalini and lead her to the highest dimension; and then to attain the knowledge of the Absolute. This is the entire purpose of the yoga system, and these practices are meant to help you toward that goal.

The science of breath actually ends with sushumna application. It is the method by which you establish harmony between the two aspects of breath. During that time both nostrils flow freely. Without sushumna application, meditation—the inward journey—becomes difficult, so you should learn the method of sushumna application. When you attempt sushumna application, ask your mind to focus at the nose bridge. Let your thoughts come and do not be afraid. You are trying to discipline your conscious mind, which is only a small part of the whole mind. When you do that, your whole being will be alert, and the whole unconscious mind will become active and bring forward many hidden and forgotten things. When this happens people often get upset, thinking that the meditation is disturbing them. But it is not the meditation that causes the disturbance, it is what you have bottled up. You have to go through that process of release in meditation therapy. This is a very good process. Let the distracting thoughts come forward, and then allow them to go. After a while a time will come when no thought patterns disturb you, and you can watch your thoughts. Then you can witness your whole life. If a disturbing thought comes, you allow it to go away.

The difference between an ordinary man and a sage is that the sage does not allow his thoughts to dwell on the negative. An ordinary man allows his thoughts to dwell aimlessly. A miserable man is one who creates a home for them. If you practice you can see the relationship between your body, breath, and mind. Your mind is your finest instrument, and yet you will finally see that the mind is not everything; something else gives power to the mind.

There is a Source that you cannot see with the mind. You leave behind the body consciousness, breath consciousness, sense consciousness, mental consciousness, and you finally go beyond all those. Then you do not identify yourself with the objects of mind or the objects of the world. When the mind attains that state of equilibrium, that is tranquility. This is the process of self-transformation. Do not become disappointed with your progress.

Sometimes a great teacher teaches his students through silence. The best and deepest of the teachings is not communicated through books, speech, or actions, but through silence. That special teaching you understand only when you are silent. The language of that silence sometimes comes to you; it is called *sandhya bhava*, the emotion of joy or equilibrium. *Sandhya* is the wedding between the day and night—the time when the day weds night, and night weds day. A teacher may ask a student, "Have you done your *sandhya?*" which means "Have you united all this and attained a state of equilibrium and joy before you meditate? Have you studied the behavior of your breath?"

If you are sensitive to all the vibrations that are going on in your body, then you can use that ability. Your sensitivity should be there; your sensitivity should be retained so that you know what is going on within. Then you know if something nice is happening in your practice and if you are progressing. There are five regular senses, but there is also a sixth sense. When you learn to direct all the five senses toward one goal or sensitivity, that state is the sixth sense. Then the sixth sense leads you to extrasensory perception. "Extrasensory" means to become sensitive to that which you normally are insensitive to, or what your senses usually are not capable of receiving. Cultivate the state in which you have withdrawn all your senses from external objects, so that you do not hear, taste, touch, see, or smell. Then the gross senses are assimilated and isolated. When that happens, all the force of energy and concentration which the mind normally uses through your senses is taken inside, and deepens your practice.

The next chapter will discuss the process of cultivating *sankalpa shakti*, determination. You need to create the resolve that you will do it, you have to do it, and you can do it—and continue to meditate. If you stumble, you will eventually learn to crawl. You will stumble again, but when you have grown you will walk, and eventually you will have the power to run or stop. To be still, be gentle to yourself.

You commit mistakes when you are ignorant. But when you have formed a habit you are not ignorant of that any longer. If you repeat a mistake again and again, a habit is formed. All your habits are repetitious, so learn not to repeat your mistakes. By not repeating whatever is wrong or unhelpful, you learn to do that which should be done. Be kind and gentle to yourself. In meditation, your body remains in a great and profound rest. You lose body consciousness because your consciousness flows upward instead of flowing downward. Meditation is a very useful and therapeutic technique. It leads you to know yourself and the unknown levels of your life; it makes you creative and brilliant. It is all in the use of the mind: if you know how to use the mind you can be successful both within and without. Life has two aspects—inner and outer—and both aspects should be touched and perfected. Then life is complete, and you can really learn to enjoy life.

CHAPTER EIGHT

The Power of Determination and Will

Step Five: Cultivating Sankalpa Shakti

When you have developed a still posture and when you have done the breathing practices, you have made the first preparations for the technique of meditation. Next you have to deal with your conscious mind. The moment you start meditating, your mind becomes very independent. The whole mind will come forward to fight with you. You also want to eventually come into touch with the unconscious. Psychologists have not yet found a way of taming the unconscious, of knowing its vast reservoir, of tapping the unconscious, the source of the infinite library within you. The unconscious mind brings up things that are of the past, such as images. In meditation you are trying to maintain that state that is in between, neither the past nor the future, but the present—this moment.

This is a battlefield within. A meditator has to face this battlefield. Meditation is not meant to be a battlefield, but you use it as a battlefield. Perhaps an image or sensation comes to mind that you decide is good—or a memory of a boyfriend whom you have forgotten long ago comes into your meditation, and then you decide that is bad. Thus you fight with yourself—all your impressions from the conscious and unconscious mind come forward. You think you are small, petty, and good for nothing—you condemn yourself because of the limitations of the mind. Therefore you need to purify the mind. You need to understand your mind and to make it one-pointed. You need to make your mind dynamic so that you do not think that you are limited. All your troubles are created in your mind. But the mind also has the capacity to lead you. It works both ways: if you do not know how to make use of your mind, it can create hellish problems for you; if you know how to use it, it can lead you to a kind of heaven. You can realize that hell and heaven are concepts created by your mind. There are no such physical places, according to yoga science. One is not punished and sent to hell; it is your mind that takes you there. Many times you experience hell here in this world—but your efforts with the mind can convert this hell into heaven, and then you can enjoy this life.

So the next step is learning to cultivate *sankalpa*, determination: that feeling "I will do it! I can do it! I have to do it!" no matter what happens. You make the effort with full determination. It is not like being forced by any outside authority; you are committing yourself, and this is your sankalpa, or resolve. You cannot attain anything without sankalpa. There are many intelligent students that do not have sankalpa, and that is why they lack confidence. They may be brilliant, but they do not have self-confidence, because they do not have sankalpa. They never disciplined themselves, so they lack sankalpa shakti.

Sankalpa shakti is a power. Without shakti you cannot be successful. All the great ones on the earth needed shakti; there was a shakti behind them to inspire them. Without inspiration even the greatest ability is scattered. If you do not have sankalpa shakti, no mere technique imparted by either your teacher or the scriptures will help you. The teacher can give you all the techniques, but if you do not have sankalpa, nothing will happen. Sankalpa is determination. Willpower is a one-pointed mind plus determination. The more one-pointed your mind and the more determined you are, the more you have willpower; if these two things are absent, then you have no willpower. Usually you do not have enough concentration or determination to develop willpower, but you can build your dynamic will, and then you can do wonders.

The first aspect of shakti that you can see is not kundalini herself, but sankalpa shakti. One aspect of the great power of manifestation and creation is actually sankalpa shakti, or determination. You can reduce a mountain into a molehill, or you can magnify that molehill into a mountain, with sankalpa shakti.

You need to decide, "I am going to sit for my meditation, and no intruding thoughts will be able to control or sway my mind. What thought can disturb my mind? I am someone; I am initiated—there is a tradition behind me. I am a human being: I have the infinite Source within me. How can a mere thought disturb me? I have allowed myself to be disturbed; that is why this thought is disturbing me. I am not going to allow this!" This is sankalpa shakti; it inspires you. Although you do not recognize it, you have immense shakti.

A snake charmer uses his shakti only for charming snakes; in a circus it is used to tame the animals; a swami uses it to tame the students. Sankalpa shakti is great and immense if you know how to use it.

There are definitely dangers, however. Sometimes you do not see your success. You are asking for rewards from your practice, but you expect these rewards without making sincere efforts. You should have one goal: that you want to experience that which is neither the past nor the future, but now. You need such determination; your determination should be firm—not that today you do it out of enthusiasm, but tomorrow you forget.

Now, when you do sankalpa, you decide that you will not allow your mind to go into its past grooves or fathom the future in imagination: you keep it in the here and now. That here and now is your mantra, your sound. It leads you not to the external world, but to the source of silence. You remember it mentally; your lips do not move, your body does not move, your breath does not create unbalanced rhythms. The mantra leads your mind to the state of silence. Mind does not want to go into silence: it has many desires to fulfill. So the mind will bring many things to your attention—and then, actually, you are not meditating. To help with this you have to have sankalpa. This is your sankalpa, which you should not forget: you decide that no matter what happens in your meditation, you will not be disturbed.

First you need to learn to make a decision; then, to have sankalpa, determination. Determination actually comes second. Of course you will fail and stumble, but that does not matter. Learn to forgive yourself for those failings. Those who do not learn to forgive themselves suffer more. They commit a mistake, and then they think that they have committed a sin. If you have committed a mistake, then decide that from now on you will not commit mistakes. Be objective and clear with yourself. First make a decision, then have determination, and then practice the correct method. In practicing, do not jump into things abruptly. Anybody who jumps into something fails. Be slow but steady in developing your practice, but be firm and determined in your commitment.

There is a story that illustrates this kind of determination.

Once a sage named Swami Rama Tirtha was traveling to the Himalayas. He started his journey in October; it was very cold and had started snowing. Many of his students said, "We will come with you." So at the city of Hardwar, the gateway to the Himalayas, he asked them to stand and count their money. He calculated that his group of twelve people had about ten lakhs of rupees (about one hundred thousand dollars). He asked, "What are you going to do with all those rupees in the Himalayas? How many blankets did you bring?" And everyone also had a large number of blankets.

Then he told them, "I do not need a group of donkeys with me. I do not want to travel with people burdened with things. Anyone who wants to walk with me, throw away your things." Nine of his followers immediately ran away, and only three remained.

They continued walking to the mountains. There it was snowing harder. Everyone said, "Sir, we are following you, but it is snowing hard!" Then Swami Rama Tirtha said to the weather, "Stop and let the sun come"—and the snow stopped and the sun shone! Swami Rama Tirtha said, "Stop as long as I am with them. You can give me this bad weather, but not them! I will protect them at all costs. Stop, snow! You can snow later!" And then the sun started shining because of Swami Rama Tirtha's sankalpa and determination.

The moment we become aware of that potential within us—that is sankalpa shakti: "I will do it, I can do it, I must do it." We all have the potential to create such determination.

Sometimes you have a problem, because you have a desire to grow but you do not have shakti, the means. The body does not remain healthy indefinitely, and when ill, it becomes a powerful distraction. Therefore the present, right now, is a great opportunity for you to start to practice. You can practice for just a few minutes every day in order to form a habit, to create new samskaras and to eliminate old samskaras: to eliminate old samskaras means to create new samskaras. If you create very powerful new samskaras, the old samskaras will vanish—but you must have determination; you must have courage; you must have sankalpa. Determination requires sankalpa, courage, and a one-pointed mind. These three will help you to eliminate the old samskaras and create a new life. Gather together all the twigs of your samskaras, light a fire, and place those samskaras in it. That is rebirth. That is what it means to be reborn, and you can do it!

Step Six: Learning to Let Go of Distracting Thoughts

So far we have discussed the importance of regularity of practice, inner dialogue, the process of developing a still body, creating serene breath, and cultivating sankalpa. The sixth step is learning to let go. The first part of meditation itself is learning to let go. Ask yourself if this thought that is coming to you is helpful for your meditation or not. Actually, no thought is helpful to you at that time, so they should be allowed to come, but you should let them go. You should develop the right attitude: let go, let go, let go. Sometimes even when you decide that you will not allow any intruding thoughts to come, the intruding thoughts come anyway, again and again; somehow you are inviting them. You should learn to let go.

Step Seven: Developing Introspection

The next step, step seven, is learning to inspect your thoughts. That is called introspection, inspection within. Usually you start to inspect within, but you do not have the capacity to continue that. You are swayed by your thoughts and identify yourself with your thought patterns. The wisdom to decide what is useful in the mind is not there, so you are controlled by your thought patterns. Inspect within to see what is good and what is not good for your practice.

If you do not have determination first, do not inspect your thoughts, because otherwise your thoughts will control you. Then you will see how easily you are distracted. Your mind will create many fantasies and images, one after another. All the images you experience are stored by you. The imagination is an image within. Whatever you have known of before, or heard, thought, studied or fantasized about—that is what you see in meditation. We think human beings have progressed, but human beings can never really think beyond their human personalities. When human beings start thinking beyond the level of the human personality, that is exploring their divinity.

No human being can really think beyond the human being. A human being is essentially perfect, having everything. That is why the human mind cannot go beyond the human mind. All great artists and thinkers finally come back to the human being, the finest of all species, the species that is considered to have been created in His own image. Human beings are actually very close to divine. God created human beings in His own image, but then man became "evil," because he forgot to salute God. When he remembers the Lord he is on the path of divinity, but when he forgets, he becomes evil.

There are really three aspects to a human being: the animal in him—which is called evil—the human aspect, and the divine. These aspects are called *tamas, rajas,* and *sattva.* The human being is like an angel that has fallen down, because he has become tamasic. He was distracted by the charms and temptations of the objects of the world, and he started to identify himself with the world, and thus forgot his essential nature. The goal of meditation is to know that essential nature.

Every time you sit to meditate, the first thing to attend to is to remember the power of your tradition, and then, when you sit in meditation, that inspires you. Examine yourself sincerely and ask yourself if you want to meditate, to explore, to know yourself, and to choose your habits. Presently you are a stranger to yourself. How can you live in the world and tolerate such agony?

Many traditions say to the student, "Know thyself," as the first step. To know thyself, there are only three schools or methods: prayer, meditation, and contemplation. At present we are discussing the process of meditation, which needs to be expanded in the waking state. You are facing yourself in that waking state, and your thought patterns are coming. You have stored them in the unconscious, and when you relax your conscious mind they come forward. Learn to allow them to let go, and then develop introspection.

Step Eight: Developing the Capacity to Witness Your Thoughts

The next step is to learn to witness your thoughts. Your thoughts are people. They are not mere thoughts; they are people within you. You are a world in yourself. You are a universe, and all your thoughts are people. Just as people are born and die, so too, thoughts are born and die. There are thoughts that create great grooves or imprints in your mind, and those thoughts are called samskaras.

You can eliminate those thoughts if you have the power, and if you know how to eliminate them; you can be free from your samskaras. If you could not do that, then human endeavor would be of no use. You can obtain freedom from your samskaras, from the impressions that you have stored in the storehouse of merits and demerits, the unconscious mind. You have the power to do that. To think that you cannot do it means that you are accepting defeat from your own self. Self-defeat is the worst part of life. After self-defeat comes self-condemnation.

To compare yourself with others is a useless competition, because you are someone who is exclusive and special. Learn to appreciate and admire yourself. Do not remain in touch only with your negativity; find out also what good qualities you have. If your habits are bad, then transform the habit patterns. The mind has a habit of going into the grooves of past experiences. When you create a new groove, the mind stops flowing into the past grooves and starts flowing in the new grooves that you have consciously created. These new grooves lead you to silence.

Your aim in meditation is to go into that silence from where wisdom flows, that fountain of life and light that flows with all its majesty. Meditation is a good thing to do; it is a great solace.

The focal point of meditation should be the breath, because the breath has both sound and light. In the next chapter we will discuss the way in which the breath has both sound and light, and how the science of sound develops.

CHAPTER NINE

The Science of Sound

*In the beginning was the Word, and the Word
was with God, and the Word was God.*
—The Gospel According to St. John

*I*F YOU STUDY all the scriptures of the world and the
philosophy of the evolution of this universe, they all
explain only so much, and then stop. The great sages
discovered in deep silence those words that are called
"unspoken words," soundless sound. Their minds were
one-pointed and inward, and their one-pointed minds
pierced through all the internal levels and picked up
those sounds from the beyond.

All the great traditions use one of three main focal
points for concentration: either a sound, syllable, or a set
of words; an image, figure, or object; or light. When you
consider sounds, there are three categories: those used in
prayers, those used in your thoughts, and those used as
mantras. A mantra is a sound, a syllable, or a set of words.
You have to train your mind to accept a particular focal
point that is not distracting, and that actually leads your
mind to become one-pointed.

To select an object or form of concentration, your
focus, you have to study your mental ability. Is your mind
inclined toward sound or music, or does something visual

attract you more? You will have to see if you react more when you see something or when you hear something. But to really select a focus for the mind, you need something that only a true teacher of the meditative tradition can give. When such a teacher imparts a sound to you, he is handing you over to an angel. He is giving an angel to you. A sound creates a form. If a sound is imparted to you, then a form is with you. If this sound is strengthened, that form is strengthened. Then you are never alone, because that form is always with you. In the beginning you and the sound are not one; you are still two in the beginning. The sound will walk with you, sleep with you, talk with you, and enjoy with you, because the sound has a form. In time, your goal is to become one with the sound.

Every thought has a form, and every sound creates a ripple that is called a thought. Each thought has a form; thus the sound and form are one and the same. Similarly, any action you perform in the external world is virtually a thought created by your sound in the ocean of bliss. We ourselves are nothing but forms created by the universal sound. Thus in the process of the creation of sound a visual form follows, because every sound has a form.

But with light there is no sound. Light does not lead you to the silence; sound leads you to the silence. That is why the great sages preferred sounds and not light as the first choice for concentration, even though light travels faster than sound. Artificial lights and images create barriers for you; they do not allow you to see the real light, which is why the Upanishads say that this jar of life is covered with something that is glittering and full of lights. It's dazzling, and our eyes are blinded, and thus we cannot see anything. These lights are so powerful that we cannot see the truth. Therefore, we seek to remove these lights. Your first job should be to free yourself from these artificial lights. You should learn to create a darkness for yourself, so that you can see the real Light.

The same is true with sounds. To hear the real sounds, the original sounds, the mother sounds, you have to protect yourself from the external sounds, otherwise your mind cannot hear them. Your brain is singing; your breath is singing; there is a music in your breath and brain. But you are not listening to it because the external sounds are keeping your mind distracted and then you are unable to hear it. You do not know the method of isolating your mind so you can listen. *Anahata nada* means "unstruck sound," beautiful music. If you hear it, you will forget all other music—but this requires discipline. The word "discipline" immediately makes you rebellious because you do not understand what discipline really means. Discipline is just regulating and directing your energy in the right direction; it is not a prison.

It is important to understand from where these sounds come, who heard them, and in what manner they were heard. In their deep meditations the minds of the great sages touched infinity, and the totality of their minds traveled in one direction, creating a state of equilibrium. When their minds attained a state of equilibrium in silence, then the sages heard these sounds. It was difficult for the sages to do it, but they knew the process of magnifying the sound.

Actually, there are two types of sounds: sound created in the external world, and sound created silently in the mind. Then, you go to the silence, you go to the silence, you go to the silence. You go to the atomic part of sound, which is very powerful. You think that this huge world of yours is powerful—but it has been discovered by science that one little particle, if it is split, is even more powerful. Your universe has no power; your world has no power: one particle can crumble your whole world, and your whole world, with all its power, cannot destroy that particle.

Thus, volume or size has nothing to do with power. The atomic source of sound lies in silence. True silence means that you gradually cut off your mind from the senses: you do not allow your senses to hear the external sounds. Then the mind hears the sound that you have stored in the impressions of the mind.

When your mind starts going inside, you will hear millions of types of sounds. You will hear and learn many languages. Some you will understand, and some you will not. That is why they talk of "speaking in tongues." This is not the ultimate knowledge; these sounds or tongues are only heard on a psychic or mental level.

All sounds originate from silence; they rise from the ocean of silence. You may discuss silence, but you have never tasted real silence. A moment of real silence is enough for one year. If someone offers me one year's pleasures or one moment of absolute silence, I will take one moment of silence, and you can keep my year of pleasure. If you put yourself into absolute silence, you will understand whatever you want. This is the great philosophy and practice of *svarodaya*.

"Svara" means a ripple of sound; "svarodaya" means the ocean. The ocean of ripples is constantly making sound. Put a tape recorder by your nose and inhale and exhale. You will hear the sound *ham-sa*, a mantra. From where did you learn this mantra? This is your breath sound. It means "I am that." The breath is singing the sound "I am that, I am that, I am that"; you are making a melody of that. The breath is constantly singing this perennial sound, *so-ham*. The science of svarodaya is a wonderful and unique subject. You can explore it your whole life, yet it will not be complete.

You need to understand the difference between word, motion, sound, and form. All sound creates form. As we said, there are two sorts of sounds: sound expanded in the external world, and sound concentrated within. Then finally there is something beyond sound: soundless sound, which is silence. So, in all, there are three ways of experiencing sound.

When sound occurs it creates a wave, a channel, or a flow. When we create a sound, it rolls, and motion has been created. The nature of sound depends on how the motion has been created. In sound therapy you use the motion of sound. If you have a knowledge of sound's motion and how to use it, sound can be therapeutic for both people and plants.

Words are used for external expression, but sound itself is actually a more powerful force. A sound can be used both internally and externally, but not words; they cannot really be used internally. When you are using a mantra correctly, it actually goes to the level of sound to become effective. When a mantra remains only a word, it is not as effective.

If you put a word or sound in proper motion, you will see that its energy flows in various ways and places. The energy itself is the same, but its pattern of flow and subtlety become different. For example, electricity can be used to create either warmth or coolness; electricity has these two qualities when it is used in certain ways.

You can understand how energy is present in the body with the help of svarodaya, the science of sound. If sound is properly taken to a subtle level, it creates a particular form that eliminates all that is not needed in that form. Medicine has the same effect. Diseases that can be cured by medicine can also be cured by light, sound, or color therapy. With the help of meditation you can use these things. If the therapist actually knows the science of the chakras, not through intellectually knowing about the chakras themselves but by knowing the science of svarodaya, he or she can understand this. By meditating you can understand this science. We will return to this point later.

Through svarodaya you can understand what the problem is and where it actually lies. If you are weak, you can develop will and strength. This occurs because of the power of sankalpa shakti, determination. If you honestly want to help somebody with all your mind, heart, and will, you can do it. Through the science of sound, the science of using words or sounds, you can help people.

Certain sounds are imparted for this. There are some related mantras that are used for various purposes. Words are used at certain points where sounds do not work. All mantras related to this plane are words—material and gross. This is a subtle technique. After the level of words, then sounds are used, and finally and most subtly, the latent part of the sounds. For example, the mantra Om is composed of three parts: A, U, M—AUM—but the finest and most powerful part of Om is actually the silence preceding and following the sound.

Just as the three schools of tantra—*kaula, mishra,* and *samaya*—are separate, there are also differences between mantras, sounds, and words. Words are used at one level; gross sounds are used at another, higher, level; and subtle sounds are used at the highest level. All the sounds and mantras end with the sound "ummmm." Any word pronounced that ends with "ummmm" has a humming sound. If you say any sound and close your mouth, and then magnify it, it becomes Om. All sounds come from

Om, and are finally annihilated and then go back into Om. The sound Om has no meaning if you do not know the silent hidden part of it. A-U-M stands for the waking, dreaming, and sleeping states, respectively; the silent part signifies the fourth state, turiya. You have to go to silence to fathom the state of turiya. You do not have to change anything else.

The world is a river, and you are standing on the bank of the river. There is a sound coming from somewhere. That sound means there is some motion. If you could hear the sound of space, you would hear the same sounds within you. A day will come, in your lifetime, when all these sounds will be recorded in outer space, and then you will recognize these sounds as already within you. That will be one of the greatest levels of wisdom that humankind will gain, by the grace of Nature and Providence.

Now, if you try to follow the sound of a river you are not actually following the sound, but you are actually following the motion of the river. This river merges into the great ocean, where there are millions and trillions of sounds mixed together—and then you are lost. This is how you are taught to study yourself in the colleges and universities. Again and again you are told to listen to others, so you do not listen to yourself. Nobody tells you to listen to yourself. You have listened to many, many things so far but nothing has happened to transform you. Learn to listen to yourself.

Commit yourself to a serious study of this process for at least a year. You have spent many hours and many years in colleges and universities; the question is whether you are willing to devote one year to the real university of knowledge within. This should be your duty, and the time you devote to this study should be very exact.

There are many levels of sounds, which range from the *muladhara* chakra at the base of the spine to the *sahasrara* chakra at the crown. There is the *anahata nada*, the sound at the heart center. *Nada* means "sound"; *anahata* means "unstruck." In anahata nada there is nothing to strike a sound, no drum or anything else—and yet a sound comes. How is that sound created?

There are actually seven key sounds, each associated with one of the seven chakras, ranging from muladhara (the root center) to sahasrara (the crown center). Those sounds create many mantras. Actually there is only one language, and that language is not spoken out loud—but if you learn that language, you can easily communicate with anyone: it is the language of the heart. When you are in a state of deep and great love with your wife or husband, you do not speak; you go to a deep silence, and there you become one. You are not alone, but all-at-one: there two become one; they are not two. Essentially they become one—because the communication is perfect. Communication starts not through your action or speech: it begins on the thought level. When you learn to communicate with yourself from this depth, there will be no problem.

The seven sounds or mantras of the chakras, if magnified, create a form. Each mantra will make a different form. But magnifying sound in the external world is not going to help you: you have to go to the source within, from which that sound comes. This form gives you a knowledge of the sound, and the sound gives you a knowledge of the silence from which all sounds come. You have to learn to go to the silence, both physically and mentally. You have to get rid of the external sounds and go beyond: you have to cross the barrier of those sounds that distract and dissipate your mind.

There is a system of going inside using sound. It is

called mindfulness. Mindfulness means attention: you pay attention to what you are doing—the first preliminary step of meditation. You cannot concentrate your mind if you are not mindful. You have to pay attention to the thing that you are doing, and you have to learn to train your mind. This is a very preliminary step, which you have to learn first.

The science of sound can heal you. A good teacher is like a very good doctor who knows the science of diagnosis, who knows where the problem lies with the student. Whether the problem is on the mental level, the physical level, the emotional level, or the level of the four primitive instincts of sex, sleep, sustenance, and survival—the teacher understands it. A good teacher will give a mantra or a sound prescription according to the diagnosis.

That sound or mantra that is meant for you should be imparted to you by the teacher. Your mantra can even be projected in such a way that it can stand before you, if really you want to evoke it, because sound means having a form, and form means a body, and that can even be a living form. Most sounds are limited in their power and effect, but a sound properly created will make all the *bijas* (seed sounds) that are found in all the chakras. The particular sound from one chakra, however, will not work for a different chakra.

In the human body there are seven levels of functioning. On each level the energy moves in a particular, characteristic way: when you examine other levels, you will see that the energy moves and behaves in different ways. So on each level the sound is different, the form is different, and its behavior is different.

If I correctly give a particular sound to a particular person for a particular chakra, then something will immediately happen. But if I give the sound for another level, it will not work; so partial knowledge is always dangerous.

Partial knowledge of the science of sound has become so cheap that everybody talks about it. Everybody talks about kundalini, and mantras, and sound—but the power is lost. Few really understand this science. One who understands the sound that is imparted knows how to use that sound. That sound and that mantra alone come forward and help you in your time of need.

What is the effect of sound on the conscious and the unconscious parts of the mind? Our conscious mind is only a small part of mind, which we use in our daily life—the part that is cultivated, educated, coached, and trained. When in the process of the death of our physical body this conscious part of the mind decays and goes with the body and breath, the unconscious part of our mind is agitated. The unconscious has a vast quantity of impressions and samskaras; the unconscious is a storehouse of accumulated impressions. If you have stored the name of the Lord or a mantra in the unconscious, it is different! Guru Nanak said this beautifully in his poetry, and all the scriptures say, "Know God, and meet God." Only one who depends on the name of God is truly satisfied and happy in the world.

However, do not use many mantras. If you try to use too many mantras, there will be a problem: they will never create a deep groove in the mind. If you have too many mantras you cannot focus your attention. That is why nuns wear a ring: they are wedded only to Christ, and no other husband is allowed. There have been many holy men in history, but if a nun has two images in her mind, then there will be two impressions in the mind—and then, during the after-life transition both impressions will be lost, and neither one will come forward. That is why it is said in the scriptures, "Do only one thing: practice, practice, practice. Go on storing, go on storing, go on storing the impressions there."

Often people think that their mantra is not helping them: they have been meditating and nothing seems to be happening. But science says that for every action there is a reaction. When you remember the mantra, what reaction do you notice? You may think that for three years you have been remembering the mantra and nothing has happened—but this is not possible, because every action has its reaction. The reaction will take place when your conscious mind fails, and then the unconscious will come forward. When you are afraid, this conscious mind does not help—but when you are in great torment, when you need great help, even in this lifetime, that unconscious impression will come forward and help. So there should not be two mantras; you should use only one. Your goal is to become one with the mantra.

The scriptures say that you are afraid because you see someone else's existence as being different from your own; that is what you are afraid of. If I am a cobra, I am not afraid of cobras! You are afraid because you acknowledge someone else's existence as different from your own—as though you believed in two existences, two entities. If you believe in only One, there will be no fear.

So it is better for you to go on creating a large accumulation of one sound in the unconscious, so that there will be only one form. If you create many sounds, there will be many forms there, because every sound has its own form. So you have to know and remember only one mantra, and that will create a great and powerful groove. When you need help, suddenly that force comes—and then you think "An angel helped me" or "Suddenly someone helped me"—but no one besides yourself helped you. It was your own faith and your mantra, deep in your unconscious mind, that projected itself to help you.

Teachers receive many letters in which people say that

on such a day something happened, and they wonder if the teacher did it. They want to believe that the teacher has flown to some place and has done something—but it is their mantra that projects itself and does it. It is you who are doing it yourself, but you do not understand how the sound is transformed into form, and how that form works.

Mantra is compact prayer. Instead of many, many words, it is a small, compact thing that has great power. While there are various mantras, you should understand your own mantra very well. Ask your teacher to explain it to you. When you receive the mantra, ask why that particular sound is given. If the teacher does not explain, you should ask, and then you should use the mantra with full determination. Using it means you are storing and restoring those impressions in the unconscious. You continue to store the impressions—and suddenly, when a time comes in which no one can help you in the external world, your mantra comes to guide you.

In meditation, the science of sound helps one to attain a state of equilibrium, and finally, beyond that, to achieve samadhi.

If you forget all the languages of your mind and remember only your mantra, you will go beyond the mind; you will remain in a state without languages, the state called samadhi. When your mind forgets all the languages, then you attain samadhi. When all the waves of the ocean of the mind form one wave, then there will be no jabbering or distraction in the mind. When all the thoughts are directed toward one wave, then those little thoughts that create ripples in the lake of the mind no longer disturb your thought. This is the way in which the mantra is used to focus and purify the mind. This process requires effort, so you must practice! If you practice, it is impossible for you not to make progress.

CHAPTER TEN

Kundalini and the Chakras

*Y*OGA PHILOSOPHY SUGGESTS that this entire universe, of which each of us is a part, is a manifestation of pure consciousness. In manifesting the universe, this pure consciousness seems to become divided into two aspects, neither of which can exist without the other. One aspect is conceptualized as masculine and is depicted as being absorbed in the deepest state of meditation—a state of formless being, consciousness, and bliss. This aspect is called Shiva.

The other aspect of the pure, nondual consciousness is a dynamic, energetic, and creative part that is called Shakti. She is the Great Mother of the universe, and from her, all forms are born. Shakti is the subtlest of forces, and she manifests herself as the entire universe—including matter, life, and mind.

When Shiva and Shakti divide or separate, it is as if they distance themselves from one another as much as they can. Shiva, or Being itself, will have nothing overtly to do with the manifestation of the universe—and Shakti, the creative principle, remains constantly busy in the ever-changing world of forms. But there is a mystery here, for Shiva and Shakti, though distant, remain essentially One. By the thinnest thread they remain united with one another—distant, yet One.

Now, certain schools of meditation suggest that the human being is a miniature universe. They say that whatever exists externally can also be found within you. The inner world is organized around the system of chakras, centers of consciousness, which link the various layers of personality. Your spine is like a pole, and there are seven major centers or chakras along that pole. When consciousness is manifested through any particular center, the result is a unique frame of reference through which you will experience the world. The uppermost center, the *sahasrara* chakra at the crown of the head, is the abode of transcendent consciousness, or Shiva. At the other end of the pole, at the root of your spinal column, there is a reservoir, a triangular cavity called a *kunda*. In the most ancient times a kunda was a bowl or vessel made for a sacrificial or ritual fire: there is a coiled fire in the kunda. That fire is a sleeping fire; it is covered with ashes, it is dormant. The *jiva*, the individual soul, suffers because that fire remains in a sleeping state.

This dormant energy resting at the base of your spine is called kundalini. Kundalini is the static support of your entire body and all its active energy forces. The tiniest portion of this energy is released in order to maintain the ordinary functioning of your body and mind. This active energy is called prana and it is distributed through the chakras and through an intricate network of 72,000 channels, or *nadis*, in the human body.

What is kundalini? Why does it lie dormant as if it were sleeping at the base of the spine? Kundalini is

Shakti. When Shakti has completed her work of manifesting the universe and has distanced herself as far as she can from her meditating Lord, she rests. Resting in the lowest part of the spine, she is called kundalini-shakti, the dormant power.

So in reality kundalini is the great fire, Shakti. She resides at the base of the spine in an energy center there called the *muladhara* chakra. If the energy of kundalini were to flow upward through the different chakras it would be called the "awakening" of kundalini. The ascending spiritual force of kundalini, however, is more than balanced by the descending energy flow of sense attractions.

The true tendency of kundalini is reflected in the name of the second chakra, the *svadhishthana* chakra. *Sva* means "in her own," and *adhishthana* means "place": *svadhishthana* means "this is her own place." The little girl, kundalini, ought to be sitting at svadhishthana, her own abode. But she was intoxicated by the wine offered by the senses; she took it in and lost her own home, and now she is not prepared to go back. The kundalini-shakti has, in a way, become intoxicated by her own creation and she has fallen to the muladhara chakra, where she is sleeping. The great spiritual fire within every human has become intoxicated with pleasures, and lies sleeping. So the *jiva*, the individual soul, cannot utilize this higher spiritual energy, and because of this, the individual soul has become a brute.

Whenever the jiva learns of kundalini-shakti, it is a great help. With the help of this force the jiva attains the highest state of consciousness, called *paramshiva*. *Shiva* is a word that means "divine"; remove "i" and it becomes *shava*, death. Without Shakti, symbolized by "i," Shiva is shava, a mere corpse.

You should make every attempt to raise kundalini and unite that energy with her Lord, Shiva. When you raise that sleeping fire of kundalini and lead her to her own home, you experience that great glittering light, that great power. Then nothing else is beautiful—because all beauty comes from there: you have found the source of beauty. The spiritual beauty of kundalini is such that once you drink of it, you are intoxicated forever.

But at the moment, you are intoxicated by another drink: the external world intoxicates people and makes them materialistic. Our modern economies lead people to such a materialistic viewpoint that if they are weak, they become workaholics. They think that the materialistic way of life is great, so they enter into a competitive lifestyle created by people who are trying to prove that they are better and more successful than one another. If you get into that competition, it never ends.

You should learn to rise to another sphere. This world of charms and temptations, like the world of matter, is one of the modifications of energy. Energy converts itself into matter, and matter into energy. But on this platform, energy, like electrons, is moving in a particular direction. You cannot change that direction. You have to learn to live in such a way that you are not affected by the motion of the world. Then you can go on to the next step.

When you rise to another dimension, you do so with the help of meditation. There is no other way to achieve spiritual awakening except through meditation, intense devotion, and right action. With the help of kundalini you will experience various indications of awakening. Your first task is to awaken kundalini. Many people awaken it unconsciously, but yogis do it consciously. Dancers, great musicians, great artists, great speakers, and great writers do it unconsciously. Their gifts do not result from personal wisdom or conscious individual power; their inspiration is a quality and a power that has been handed to them. Traditionally we say that kundalini-shakti contains not only latent energy but also latent memories, both personal and transpersonal. The modern way of expressing this is through the term "the unconscious." Like Shakti, the unconscious is conceived as a vast unknown power. When you have opened some access into the unconscious you become energetic, insightful, and creative. So it is with the latent power of Shakti: those who transform this spiritual force from its latent to its active form experience the full spiritual transformation of their personality.

Kundalini-shakti is the finest force that is in the individual soul. When you depart from your body, that latent shakti is there. Propelled by the energy of kundalini and the samskaras of the unconscious mind, each individual finds a new body. This is called *janman*, or birth.

Similarly, you start every day after a "death" of eight hours that you call sleep; you wake up again and are reborn. Then you complete the work that you left behind the previous day. There are many things you must do— but if you only complete your worldly task of earning the means to survive and live comfortably, and do not know how to apply the means to attain the ultimate purpose of life, then worldly success is not of much benefit. Be aware of the real goal and utilize all your means to attain it. If you have built your sankalpa shakti—which is actually the first shakti—and have learned to talk to and use your mind, then you can do it. With the help of kundalini-shakti you can go to the summit—the abode of Shiva— and experience that great perennial peace.

So how do we awaken the kundalini-shakti? We awaken it in two stages: first by actually awakening it, and second by learning to lead it. To awaken kundalini there is a very small and succinct technique: to awaken the fire, you blow on it. The sound that arises with that blowing is the mantra so-ham, so-ham, so-ham.

There are two sounds in the breath. The two sounds, "so" and "ham," are actually the two sounds of your breath. "So" is the sound heard when you inhale; the exhalation creates the sound "ham." *So-ham* means "I am that." You breathe that great cosmic energy, the energy that gives us birth, and through that breath you are linked to the Divine. There is only one force from which we are receiving energy—we are related as brothers and sisters; we are children of one eternity. We forget that fact, and acknowledge only our egos. We develop only our egos, and that is why we suffer, why we hate and hurt others. When you are aware that there is only one source of energy, only One who is father to all, then you will love your fellow beings because you will realize that your existence and their existence are from the same source. This is the essence of the teaching of kundalini.

The awakening of kundalini is often depicted as a sudden, intense, earth-shattering experience. Certainly, the vision of Saul on the road to Damascus is an example of spiritual awakening that has those qualities. But such experience is rare. It is more usual for tiny bits of this energy to be released as bursts of enthusiasm, peak experiences, a sense of well-being, and similar changes in consciousness. This is very much like what happens in psychotherapy as bits of the unconscious are brought into awareness.

Now, many schools of meditation say the student should systematically learn all about the chakras. Other schools say that that will waste one's whole life, and that one should know about the chakras only in sufficient detail so that, in meditation, when flashes come from various chakras, or the thought patterns, forms, and images of the chakras arise, you will understand their meaning; if you do not, those images will distract your mind. So to avoid distraction, you learn that a particular image comes from one chakra, or a particular sound comes from another chakra, or a fragrance comes from still another chakra. Then, when you are meditating on a chakra and a flash comes, or you suddenly start smelling a fragrance, you will know on which chakra you are really focusing. This information helps you understand your practical experience.

From the perineum in the pelvic area to the medulla oblongata, there are six knots or centers. These are the six lower chakras located along the spinal column. Their job is the distribution of impulses.

In considering these chakras, students want to know what they are and where they are located. If you close your eyes, you will not see any images of flowers or petals—if you do, it is only because you have seen images in a book, and you remember them. You do not really understand the purpose or meaning of these images experientially. Do not become fascinated by these pictures. These geometrical figures, these lotuses, are just symbols; the chakras themselves are not actually like that. A symbol is a representative of something more than itself. The symbol is a form of sound. The sounds heard at the various chakras were heard by the great sages, and then passed on to their students.

When you meditate on the spinal cord, do not visualize the chakras as located in the front; they are in your spinal column. There is one main *nadi*, or channel of energy, called *sushumna*. Your chakras, the spheres of energy positioned along this central channel, are each in motion.

In the scriptures three *bindus* are described. A bindu means a dot, circle, or hole. A bindu can become a circle, a center—or a hell-hole. You can interpret it in whichever way you think of it. Of the three bindus, one is blue, one is red, and one is white. These three bindus—the upper, middle, and lower—are focal points for the mind in meditation. These bindus are related to the chakras; they connect one region with another. The knowledge of the bindus is imparted by the yogis when the student is ready to receive it. The bindus are called *rakta*, *sveta*, and *nila*. Teachers understand the mental conditions of their students and thus prescribe one of these bindus. Finally the teacher leads the student to pierce the pearl of wisdom and go beyond to the Limitless.

The chakras themselves all have a color, a shape, and a *bija*. The bija is a seed sound. All sounds come from the source of sound, where all mantras reside. Those mantras or bijas have been given to us by those fortunate few masters who first experienced them.

The powers associated with the chakras are just signs and symptoms to tell you how much ability and capacity you have developed. They do not lead you anyplace—they are actually disturbances and distractions. They can give you confidence, but if you are interested in miracles or *siddhis* (powers) they can distract and destroy you. Sometimes swamis or yogis receive siddhis, such as extrasensory perception. They may attain a siddhi on the psychic level, the mental level, or the spiritual level—but if they become distracted by these, then their progress is finished.

To genuinely awaken kundalini you must prepare yourself. Without patiently purifying your mind and strengthening your capacity, the flood of energy that occurs with the awakening of this latent power would be deeply disturbing and disorienting. The teacher who truly represents a tradition that teaches methods to awaken kundalini will never fully reveal these to an unprepared student, but will do his best to prepare the student. Preparation for awakening kundalini is more important than awakening kundalini.

The teacher sees what you need, where your mind is focused, and gives you a practice. If you are not honest with yourself, however, you cannot make progress. What is important is honesty—not just to your teachers, but most importantly to yourself. When you do your practice, you should always sit in the way and at the time you were told. You need to be honest with yourself in making a commitment that for so many months, no matter what happens, you will devote yourself to meditating at exactly the same time. If you do not do your practice faithfully, mere intellectual understanding of the chakras is of little value.

The question of what is prominent in your life matters a great deal. Whatever is prominent in your life intensifies in meditation. Whether you are lusty, greedy, or lacking preparation; whether you are honestly and sincerely doing your practice—your tendencies and traits will become magnified. If you are irresponsible in managing your sexuality, that tendency will also increase, because in meditation your mind expands.

You need to examine honestly what is in your mind. Be honest with yourself. Do not meditate if you are being hypocritical and are just sitting and punishing yourself. If you do something honestly in the external world, then you reap the fruits according to the intensity and the one-pointedness of your action. The mind strengthens whatever particular desire is already there. So first, the mind should be emptied of those desires. There should be only one desire, the desire for meditation, the desire to go deep inside. At first you will fail to achieve it, but that does not matter; you should not give up. If you give up, you will only waste time in meaningless experiments and will gain nothing of value.

There are different sounds produced in the body. The brain sings in one way; the mind sings in another (the mind can create any tune for you). The nervous system sings in yet a different way. There is a network of 72,000 *nadis*, or energy channels, in the human body. A perfectly accomplished yogi is supposed to know all of them. Actually, however, teachers eventually say, "There is no need to count all the leaves of the tree; just pluck the fruit, eat them, and go away." If you go to a tree that bears a lot of fruit, but start counting how many leaves are on the tree, you will be deprived of the pleasure of eating the fruit. In your studies you sometimes waste your energies. You pay attention to issues like the number of stars in the sky. A good student should be like a bee that not only knows how to collect the essence from many different flowers, but also knows how to convert it into honey. A good *sadhaka*—seeker, spiritual student— should be discriminating, like a bee, and take the essence from many different experiences and then convert it into spiritual knowledge. That is called *mahavidya*, the great knowledge.

The student who is taught mahavidya knows how to derive good qualities from everything. There is nothing in the world that is totally negative. Chemicals such as arsenic, sulfuric acid, and potassium cyanide can kill you, but they also can be used as medicines. If you know how to use things, nothing will kill you—if you do not use something properly, however, it will definitely harm you. Similarly, the study of the chakras and kundalini should be used correctly.

As you progress in your study you will learn that there is an even deeper science than the science of chakras, though it is not explained in any manual. It is what the gurus impart to their disciples not through books or words but only through silence. Gurus, those great kind ones, impart the best of their knowledge in silence. When you are in silence they communicate with you through silence and in silence. For the student whose mind is in tune, that teaching is the finest of teachings. This silent communication can happen no matter where you are physically, whether you are ten thousand miles away or very close. This science is imparted only to those who are very well prepared.

Muladhara Chakra

The *muladhara* chakra, the first chakra, is located at the coccyx, the group of fused vertebrae at the base of the spine. The symbol for this chakra is a triangle facing downward—not upwards, as some books show it. The triangular flow is actually downward. The triangle is inside a square, which represents the earth, or solid matter. The color of the muladhara chakra is yellow. Its element is earth, and smell is its sense. It is said that whenever you meditate and have a sense of smell, it comes from the muladhara chakra.

In yoga philosophy the entire universe is thought to be formed from combinations of five basic elements, or *bhutas*. Each combination has a different proportion of primordial matter *(prakriti)* and consciousness *(purusha)*. Each *bhuta* is associated with a human cognitive sense. We have noted, for example, that the sensation of any sort of fragrance, the object of the sense of smell, is related to the muladhara chakra. Using the power of this chakra you can separate various scents and then understand how each fragrance was derived. You can tell from which flower a fragrance comes—it is actually possible to have that power.

The muladhara chakra is associated with the earth element. The focus of the mind when it manifests through this chakra is on the material plane of existence. Such basic concerns as material and physical security are important here.

The earth element is associated with the sense of smell because all fragrances come from the earth, not from the sky; there are no flowers in the sky; they grow only on the earth. It is interesting to consider the nature of plants. The seed of a plant goes into the ground, the earth, and forms roots. Another part of the plant grows out of the ground. These are the two important parts of plants. We human beings do not grow our roots in the earth in the same way that a tree does; we grow our roots in attachments to external objects. In this context the word "attachment" has more than one meaning. Most often in yoga, "attachment" has a negative connotation: it conveys a meaning of spiritual bondage. But a tree grows in attachment in a positive way as its roots grow down in the soil. If the roots are not strong, there will be no fruit. The whole stem will crumble if there is no root; that is very important. The roots of a tree are like the root lock, or *mula-bandha*. This tree of life, this pillar that has its crown at the top of the head, will crumble in meditation if there is no root lock.

The earth-plant plane is very important; it provides a foundation. You should understand this foundation within your personality. Anything related to the earth or to your earthly or sensual desires or pleasures comes from this root, the muladhara chakra.

The energy or prana that flows at the muladhara chakra has a particular motion, and creates a particular sound. The principle here is that movement of any kind creates sound. If there were no flow of prana there would be no sound. This whole universe, within and without, is a ripple, and ripples create sound.

The sound created at the root center is "lam." Now "lam" is, itself, a magnified sound. It arises from silence. When the potential energy of that silence becomes manifested at the root center, it forms the bija "lam."

At some point in a student's practice, the mind and the sound become one. Then you want to lead your mind to a deeper level. At the muladhara chakra you experience the sound "lam," but knowing that sound in its magnified form does not really help you. If you want to go to the subtler aspect of "lam" then you, like the sages, must go to the state of silence.

There you see that there is no drum, no one who is striking a drum—but a voice is coming from the silence: the voice of the silence. From this silence flow all the rivers that create the great *nada*, the inner ocean of sound, which is always in wavelike motion. There, in silence, you will find out what "lam" really means.

When "lam" expands itself it actually creates a symbol. In the same way that vibrations of sound can be used to create patterns in a thin layer of sand, the sound "lam" creates a form. Out of silence comes sound, and out of sound comes form.

You can meditate at the root center for particular purposes. Some do worship (*yajna*) and ritual at the muladhara chakra by using the bija "lam" in their meditation. "Yajna" is a wonderful word to understand; it means both internal worship and external worship. In ancient times, eighteen participants were needed to perform a yajna: these eighteen are the five subtle senses, the five gross senses, the five pranas, the two breaths, and the mind—eighteen in all. So a human being is constantly worshipping: in this field of the body, all eighteen are performing yajna constantly, keeping the fire of life alive.

Any disease related to your senses can be cured or healed by doing yajnas. You actually have ten senses: smelling, touching, tasting, seeing, and hearing are the five subtle senses; and there are another five senses, called the active or gross senses: the mouth, hands, feet, and the two gates—the front and rear gates. Diseases related to these senses can be healed by doing yajnas.

If you have the desire for anything in the external world, you will gain it or attain it with the help of the sound "lam." You can attain great wealth—or what you may call wealth—such as money, gold, or even property. From the worldly viewpoint you can become very rich by meditating on this chakra with a particular mantra. That is what this sound does—provided it is known at its origin and not through its external form.

The root center, however, is a lower chakra. It is associated with sensual enjoyment. When you meditate on this chakra it will create a great and intense sensitivity in your sexual activity. If your mind goes into the grooves of sexuality all the time, you are focusing on the muladhara chakra. Preoccupations with sex, wealth, and other material desires are not helpful to aspirants, and therefore the muladhara chakra is rarely given to students as their center of concentration.

Svadhishthana Chakra

Svadhishthana is the second chakra. Although kundalini resides in the muladhara chakra, actually her home is not there. When you begin to experience kundalini you will find her in her real nature not at the base of the spinal column, but at svadhishthana chakra, "her own abode." She is at muladhara chakra only because she is in a sleeping state. You cannot really study kundalini when she is fast asleep. You cannot really study kundalini at all; you can only worship and adore her. If by chance a spark comes and you are able to use the sound of your mantra to blow away the ashes that cover that fire, then the warmth of that fire will give you the wisdom of this center. If you can awaken kundalini and are able to lead her to svadhishthana, you will then experience the warmth. The intoxication of kundalini is such an intoxication that once you drink of it you are intoxicated forever. You will not wreck your liver or nervous system, however, by becoming aware of the intoxication of kundalini in svadhishthana. When you take kundalini to her own abode at svadhishthana, there she becomes conscious of her family members, and she decides not to leave her home. This innocent and beautiful girl, full of power, then awakens.

The shape of this chakra is not a triangle: it is in the shape of a half moon. This chakra governs the sense of taste. The substance or element is water. At the first center it is solid matter, but here at the second, it is water. There is water around the earth, and also in the human body. Most of the human body, and most of the surface of the earth, is actually water. You cannot live without water; it is the essence of life. Diseases that are related to the fluid systems in the body, such as blood or circulatory problems, can be helped by focusing on this center.

There is tremendous power here at svadhishthana. The sound or bija of svadhishthana is "vam," and the color is blue or bluish. It is not pure blue, but is exactly the color of the ocean. Whenever there is a flash of yellow light during meditation, it indicates the energy of the muladhara chakra; if there is a flash of blue light, it means there is energy at svadhishthana.

There are sexual diseases that are definitely related to this center and to the power of kundalini. Herpes is one of them. Like the kundalini that remains in a latent state and then rises, herpes similarly oscillates between latency and active expression. Herpes can be cured, but if it is in a latent state, it often comes back in women when they have their menstrual period because during that time their immune system is weaker.

Manipura Chakra

The next chakra is the manipura chakra. It is located at the navel center. Its form is a triangle pointing upwards. At the manipura chakra the sound is "ram" and the element is fire. Fire controls this particular dimension. It also governs the sense of sight. The light of this chakra is red. If you never have an experience of red light, it means that you need warmth in your body, and you are losing the warmth of life. There is something wrong—your digestion is poor and your gastric fire is not working adequately.

The colors that you experience in meditation tell you about the state of your body and mind. They are symptoms that tell you that you need to work on something.

We tell students who are of weak constitution to concentrate on the manipura chakra. The fire within you at manipura chakra is responsible for maintaining you on the earth; It is a very prominent and important chakra. The manipura chakra is called the *khanda*, that which controls the entire lower hemisphere. It assists in maintaining the health of the entire body through its close relationship with many of the body's organ systems. For example, the fire of this center aids digestion and is involved with nourishment, warmth, and the energy of the body. This chakra also controls both digestive fluids—gastric fluid and saliva.

The extent of the interrelationship between this chakra and other organ systems is interesting. To maintain a healthy digestive fire you must, of course, eat balanced, nutritious foods. Preparation before eating is very important. Do not eat if you are not calm. It is because of the interaction between emotions and digestion that it is unhealthy to fight at the dining table.

If the activity of the right vagus nerve is disturbed by poor breathing, then the health of the body, heart, and digestive system are all imperiled. You can improve your digestion with the help of breathing exercises. Exercises such as even breathing have been very therapeutic in aiding digestion.

Another system in your body related to the manipura chakra is responsible for the cleansing process: this is the eliminatory system. It has four main routes: the pores, lungs, bowels, and kidneys. Just as you take care of the nourishing and digestive system, so you should also take care of the eliminatory system. If you do not take care of the cleansing system, then no matter how you nourish your body you cannot really be healthy. The pores should secrete well, the lungs should function well, the bowels should move well, and the kidneys should also function well—then you will be truly healthy. Concentrating on the manipura chakra is unique and special for the sake of one's health: it aids in maintaining all these functions. Therapy makes use of this fire in the lower hemisphere at the manipura chakra. If you go closer, closer, and still closer to a fire, a time comes when you cannot go any nearer or you will be burned. By concentrating on the manipura chakra you can create heat in the internal solar system. There are some external practices that can be done to do this, just as there are external practices for *trataka*, gazing. These practices allow you to strengthen the solar fire. In the case of many illnesses, if the therapist or doctor can encourage the patient to do *agni sara*, the solar plexus exercise, it will be very useful.

To correctly diagnose your own illnesses you should learn to meditate on the manipura chakra. If you then want to understand those illnesses in detail, you can go to your doctor. You can diagnose and heal yourself in some circumstances.

Anahata Chakra

The next center is the heart chakra, the anahata chakra. It is located in the center of the chest, between the two breasts. Its element is air, and it governs the sense of touch. The color of the anahata chakra is a smokey color, like smokey topaz. It is symbolized by two intersecting triangles, one pointed upward, the other pointed downward. The sound or bija of the heart center is "yam." This sound originates at the anahata chakra and then flows both upward and downward. The anahata chakra is another powerhouse—a powerhouse of emotions. Emotional problems can be controlled and eliminated by concentration at the anahata chakra. Meditation on the anahata chakra can be a wonderful, devotional experience. When properly channeled, emotions can lead you to a deep state of ecstasy. For example, sometimes when you are listening to good music, you suddenly fall into a state of ecstasy. With the help of sound you can easily attain this state, provided you know how to do it.

This is also the place where your mind resides during sleep. Concentrating here makes you drowsy and can put you to sleep. During meditation you want to remain fully conscious, with no mental strain. If you are not having a good meditation, do not do it; simply get up and go away. Do not fight with your mind during meditation. If the mind decides not to meditate, do not try to do it at that time. If you fight with the mind, you will be sitting and fighting, and that will not be meditation. You will be asking your mind to quiet down while the mind is focused on its unfulfilled desires—that simply creates conflict.

Fire has the capacity to burn off impurities. When gold is put into a fire, it shines. When you put your mind into the fire, it loses all its gross impurities. There is no question of lower and higher chakras. You have to systematically study the practices to understand yourself. If you are going to be a great teacher, therapist, or doctor, you should learn yourself what happens when you put your mind into the fire. The fire at the anahata chakra is not the fire of knowledge; that is another chakra. It is a fire that makes you healthy—giving you physical and emotional health, vigor, and energy.

As indicated, the anahata chakra is symbolized by two triangles, one superimposed on the other. The upward-pointing triangle signifies fire. The second triangle points downward. Flames travel upwards, not downward;

sexual energy travels downward. At the anahata chakra these two forces meet—the upper hemisphere and the lower hemisphere. That is why there are two triangles. This symbol is called the Star of David in Judaism. It also is similar to a cross, where two poles meet. If, through experience, you understand this union of two forces, you will not have any problem understanding symbols. You can understand all the symbols accepted by any religious tradition if you understand the anahata chakra.

Concentration on the anahata chakra is therapeutic for all emotional purposes. For therapeutic purposes, doing alternate nostril breathing from the anahata chakra to the crown chakra is very helpful.

Vishuddha Chakra

The fifth chakra, the vishuddha chakra, is located at the pit of the throat. It is associated with creativity and with the creative arts, such as dancing and music. Its sound is "ham." Its element is space, symbolized by a circle. Its color is blue. It governs the sense of hearing.

This chakra functions at the gateway of the body called the throat. Here nourishment is taken in, and speech and song are expressed outwardly. There are two unique yoga techniques that have therapeutic value to relax the tension of this area: the first is the upper wash, and the second is devotional chanting.

Ajna Chakra

The ajna chakra is the sixth chakra, and it is very important. It is located at the space between the two eyebrows. Its color is clear. Its element is the mind. It is beyond the gross elements. It is the gateway to the city of life. Using the little actual spiritual knowledge that you receive here, you can be creative in the external world. You also can be creative in the internal world at the spiritual level. If spiritual understanding is given to you, it comes through the ajna chakra.

The mind likes to travel. The mind refuses to concentrate or meditate on one thing. It can take any shape, but the mind itself does not want to be limited or defined. It is very independent but it always needs an object to lean on or focus on: it takes off, and then it comes back; it wants to go here and there. Mind needs a focal point, and when the mind is focused and directed, it becomes very dynamic and creative. The bija for the ajna chakra is "Om."

Sahasrara Chakra

The final chakra is the sahasrara chakra, the thousand-petaled lotus. It is located at the crown of the head. It is this whole universe, and above and beyond that: life here and hereafter. At the sahasrara chakra all limitation and dualities have been transcended. It represents the state of cosmic consciousness. There are no colors, elements, or senses associated with this chakra, because it is the state beyond.

The Chakras and Therapy

All the chakras have a specific domain. As you become aware of the organ system and emotions related to each chakra you can begin to diagnose disturbances in the normal patterns of those centers. This method of diagnosis is unique. A good doctor or therapist can diagnose diseases and problems in a profound way. When someone who is completely selfless and compassionate tries this method, it never fails.

In this method of diagnosis the doctor does not concentrate on the patient's chakras—the doctor concentrates on his or her own! This method is called intuitive diagnosis. In the process of intuitive diagnosis you will learn to understand the distributing centers, or chakras, that send energy and sensations from one part of the body to another.

To understand how this method works you should think a little about what it means to diagnose something. How does a therapist make a diagnosis? One of the rules of therapy between therapist and patient is that the two persons must be honest with one another. Sometimes the therapist must say something to the patient that he does not want to say, but the contract between the two is to be honest in expressing themselves. If the patient can feel secure enough that he can openly express himself, usually the therapist can help him. Thus a very close relationship develops between therapist and client.

This close relationship becomes one in which the therapist's mind can operate in a very accurate and intuitive way. How does this happen? It is easy to explain. I breathe the same air that you breathe. If you are sitting next to me and are deprived of air, then automatically I too will be unable to breathe. Providence is not doing anything to me, but Providence is keeping breath from you—so we are both affected because there is only one center from which we both gain our energy. We are very close; we are brothers and sisters. We are twin souls. Actually it is even more than that, more even than the idea that we are one. Now if I remain in an objective state of mind toward my own body while being in such complete empathy with you, I can diagnosis your problem by examining my own centers of consciousness. Only self-ishness on the part of the therapist limits the mental sensitivity and creates blocks.

As a therapist you must learn not to identify yourself with the patient. There are patients who are considered to be uncommunicative; they cry more than they speak. If you make the mistake of identifying with the patient, you will get tired and sick. You can counsel many patients, but you will lose the capacity to counsel if you do not remain objective or if you start identifying yourself with them.

If you cannot understand the problem because the symptoms are similar to many diseases, and traditional clinical diagnosis fails, then diagnose intuitively. Once the diagnosis is accurate, you can treat the patient. When diagnosing intuitively, you will also know if a patient is going to survive or not.

In intuitive diagnosis you do not have to make an effort. It is purely numerical, like counting from one to eight. It does not require spiritual wisdom. It is a process, a method; if you know the methodology, you can use it. You can do it both consciously or unconsciously. Edgar Cayce did it unconsciously. Somehow he came in touch with that ability in himself. He would lie down, become unconscious, and then diagnose people's illnesses; at the same time he would prescribe a remedy. That is an unconscious use of this ability. This method, however, also can be a conscious method. The process of intuitive diagnosis is a wonderful process which requires no effort from the mind. It is a very simple, spontaneous process in which there are no mistakes. A human being who has learned this can be successful about ninety-nine percent of the time. It is not possible to be one hundred percent perfect because there is only one Perfection, and no one can be perfect except that Absolute One. So if you learn to use this system, about one percent of the time you will be unsuccessful and disappointed, but most of the time you will succeed. Remember, for intuitive diagnosis you do not meditate or concentrate on the patient's chakras or plexuses, as medical science calls them. Rather, you concentrate on your own. To be aware of any disease related to matter, you concentrate on the muladhara chakra. For diseases related to the liquids in the body, concentrate on the svadhishthana chakra. Next is the very important chakra the manipura chakra: concentration on this chakra will lead to intuitive diagnosis of diseases related to the body's fire and digestive systems.

Sometimes medicines are ineffective in treating certain diseases. Then it is helpful to know something about the solar science. The solar science is also unique; it is a science of colors. This is a wonderful and unique subject. You can explore it your whole life, yet it will not be complete. To master it, you need to understand the difference between word, motion, sound, and form. Through the solar science you can use light and color therapy. You can use various colors of water, energized by sunlight at different times of the day, in a place where you have enough sun. Water receives and stores light well. You can see the light of the sun reflected in many vessels, and it gives the same effect. You can keep the vessels of water, and you can still see the sun in them. The effect will be the same. In water of different colors, the light of the sun's rays will have different effects. All the possible colors are contained in sunlight. This science is called the solar science.

The body produces heat using its "solar system" at

the manipura chakra. In this solar science there are special practices involving certain postures and breathing rhythms that are taught in the Himalaya Mountains. For example, we are taught to sit in a certain posture and then do specific breathing rhythms that can produce such heat that the entire body will perspire, even in a cold climate. Using such practices one can maintain the health of the body even in adverse conditions.

Ideally your mind should control your body perfectly: if you want to cry, your body should cry; if you want to smile, your body should do that immediately. If your mind works well, your body should be able to express whatever your mind wants. Then perfect coordination exists between body and mind. To have perfect health one needs coordination between many things: nutrition, digestion, elimination, and regeneration. A well-coordinated body is a healthy body. Sometimes people seem to be healthy but they are not actually well-coordinated. A body that is not coordinated is unhealthy and sick.

With the help of the science of color therapy you can learn to treat many diseases. In the past therapists used large pans like solar collectors to store the energy from the solar system, in the same way you do today with solar energy. To create medicines they used pure water, sunlight, and various colors. The pans of water, or sometimes costly bottles of water, were used therapeutically to store and radiate the solar energy.

To understand this better, you can try it. Take a large bottle of colored water and keep it somewhere where there is enough sun. Expose it till it deepens in color. That color will deepen if it is exposed to sun for twenty-eight hours. It should have a full twenty-eight hours of sun. When there is no sun, cover the bottle of water with a blanket. Once such water is prepared you can store it in a refrigerator; its effectiveness will not be destroyed or its potential lost. If it is exposed for six or eight hours to the sun, it should be covered with something opaque so that the quality of the water is not destroyed. It should not be exposed to heat or to other light, such as lamps. It is to be kept in the refrigerator or exposed to the sun alone. This is the way they prepared certain medicines out of pure water energized by the rays of the sun.

Normally, colors that are exposed to the sun will fade. But in twenty-eight hours that colored water will change and deepen in color. Once that water has had enough of the sun's rays, it creates a new radiation and is therapeutic for many purposes, but best for the skin and asthma. Many diseases—for example, leprosy—can be cured by that colored water because it is so powerful and full of energy. The important sign is that its color, instead of fading, deepens. Conducting color therapy by using a colored lamp can also be done, but it is not totally safe and can even be dangerous. Sound therapy is even more subtle than color therapy and is a deeper science.

A good teacher is like a good doctor who knows diagnosis, who knows where the problem lies with the student, whether on the mental level, the physical level, the emotional level, the level of desire, or the level of the four primitive fountains: food, sleep, sex, or fear for survival. A well-trained teacher will prescribe a therapeutic sound or color according to that diagnosis, and that sound or color can definitely heal.

CHAPTER ELEVEN

Exercises

$\mathcal{T}$HE WORD *YOGA* is used to mean "union." When your individual soul unites with the Cosmic Soul, when you are one with the Absolute, that is yoga. In the state of samadhi you are fully conscious; you are free. Your consciousness is completely expanded. In sleep you are there, but you are not conscious of it. It is a state very close to samadhi. Samadhi is that state of equilibrium that you attain through deep meditation. You remain fully conscious and aware, but your state of mind attains equanimity and equilibrium. In deep sleep you are very close to samadhi, but you are not conscious. There is a method called yoga nidra in which you can have conscious sleep. Yoga nidra is a state between sleep and samadhi.

It is a half-sleep and half-waking state: it is not a waking state, and it is not really a sleep state. It is a state where you can gain complete rest and a little bit of sleep, but remain fully awake. It is very beneficial. In it you will rest fully, experience good sleep, and also have a good state of consciousness. This practice is used by yogis to know or learn something that they ordinarily cannot know in the waking state. They use it to become aware of many things. Great men like Mahatma Gandhi, Napoleon, and Raja Ranjit Singh were not aware that they were practicing yoga nidra, but actually they approached this state of sleepless sleep. It alone could give them enough time to work and not waste many hours, as ordinary people usually do.

Yoga nidra is a state of conscious sleep in which you can record what is going on. It is one of the finest and most beautiful exercises; it will help you to solve problems and give you solutions to questions where the answers are consciously unknown to you. The proper technique is important, but in addition to understanding the technique, you need to have strong determination and desire.

There is a fine demarcation between yoga nidra and samadhi. In the method called yoga nidra you are in deep sleep, yet you are recording within—you switch on your inner tape recorder to record. You can see wonders and talk in many languages, a phenomenon that can be scientifically observed. If this practice is continued you can register what happens inside; words, sentences, paragraphs, and passages will not be forgotten. Whenever they are needed they can be recalled. During that time you are very powerful and your mind is greatly expanded, yet your mind is completely under your control. There are two types of yoga nidra. In one, you can even communicate with others while remaining in deep sleep.

I demonstrated yoga nidra at the Menninger Foundation in Topeka, Kansas. [See *Beyond Biofeedback* by Elmer and Alyce Green.] I showed how to be in a deep sleep yet remain fully conscious, recording everything. During that time, consciousness magnifies and records well. If in my waking state I want to do something about which I have no knowledge, or if I cannot find a solution with my physical mind and brain, then I go to sleep in yoga nidra, find the answer, and come back to wakefulness with the exact information.

In yoga nidra you can record those things that you cannot receive in the conscious state. When one cannot register something properly in the waking state, they can go into yoga nidra to register it. Yoga nidra is used to develop that wisdom that cannot be developed otherwise. If you really want to strengthen intuition you should practice yoga nidra. Normally your mind does not have sufficient capacity because you have cultivated only a small part of it, but in yoga nidra your field goes beyond the waking, dreaming, and sleeping states. The mind is not in the fourth state, turiya, itself, but it is between turiya and sleep. That is called yoga nidra.

The difference between sleep and yoga nidra is consciousness. When you sleep it is customary for you to do so unconsciously. That is why you do not really enjoy the experience. But sleep should be enjoyed; food should be enjoyed—all the primitive fountains can be enjoyed when you experience them consciously. You do things out of habit and so you do not enjoy anything. When you and your partner have sex together, often one of you is dissatisfied because it is not done consciously.

But yoga nidra is conscious. It is a conscious sleep. In yoga there is nothing that puts you into an unconscious state, except one *kriya* called *plavini kumbhaka*, in which the yogi consciously passes out. Sometimes children like to do this in play by spinning. Hypnotists try to create that state, but hypnosis is very dangerous because the state is reached under someone else's guidance. Yoga nidra, however, is the safest practice in the world. There is no method better than yoga nidra, yogic sleep.

During sleep you will find that you do not breathe very deeply; you breathe shallowly. If you are a yogi, you breathe in a fine way. The way a person breathes is related to heart function. A shallow, irregular breathing pattern injures your heart during sleep; you don't gain rest. With yoga nidra you can be helped. Many people breathe poorly; they do not breathe evenly during sleep. It is injurious for the heart to have a deep inhalation and a very shallow exhalation. That period of life that is meant for total rest should not be injurious; both the body and the heart should receive rest. When this shallow and irregular breathing occurs, the heart is injured because the pumping station must change its rhythm repeatedly. When you are breathing incorrectly, there is also a marked difference in the heart's efficiency at pumping the blood.

Thus the heart goes through needless stress. The motion of the lungs is related to the heartbeat, and the blood supply is also related to that. The right vagus nerve, which is responsible for digestion, is also involved. So the entire system becomes irregular in its functioning. But you can regulate it: yoga nidra helps you with this problem.

In yoga nidra you do not lose consciousness, yet your whole body, mind, and nervous system, as well as both kinds of muscles (smooth and striated), obtain complete rest. You will gain control over the voluntary and involuntary nervous systems. If you really know what yoga nidra is and are able to do it, then you do not need sleep. If you sleep deeply for three hours and compare that with yoga nidra, you will find yoga nidra far superior to three hours of ordinary sleep. In a book called *Kumbhakarana*

Ramayana it is mentioned that one great yogi used to sleep for six months, and would then remain awake for six months. Only advanced yogis can do such practices; these intense practices are conducted and practiced when you have adequate time. In a busy schedule like yours, practicing a kind of yoga nidra in which you do not have to go so deep is more practical. Yoga nidra is a powerful practice that will be a great help to you.

There are two exercises related to yoga nidra that are also very helpful. The first is the Sixty-one Points exercise. It is one of the finest exercises in relaxation, breathing, and meditation. If you do this exercise regularly it will be very beneficial. The results of this practice can be clinically examined. Those who are suffering from high blood pressure, high blood sugar, peptic or gastric ulcers, problems with blood circulation, or tension and stress will see improvements after practicing this exercise.

Sixty-one Points Exercise

To do the Sixty-one Points exercise, lie down in *shavasana*, the corpse pose, with a small pillow under your head. Begin with overall body awareness, making sure

Shavasana—The Corpse Pose

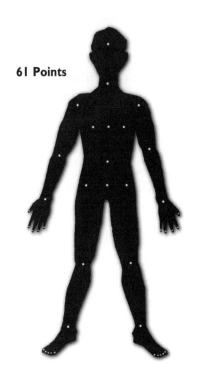

61 Points

that you are positioned correctly in shavasana—with your feet spread, the toes pointed outward, the hands a little bit away from the body, palms up, eyes and lips gently closed, and the tongue relaxed at the roof of the mouth. From an overall body awareness, turn your awareness to your breath, noticing each inhalation, each exhalation, and the transition between the two. Let the breath flow without pauses, jerks, or noise. Let the length of the inhalation equal the length of the exhalation, and let both be done to your own comfortable capacity.

Take your awareness to each named part of the body and relax that part of the body. Start with number 1, the center of the forehead; go to number 2, the throat center at the pit of the throat; number 3, the right shoulder joint; 4, the right elbow joint; 5, the right wrist joint; 6, the tip of the right thumb; 7, the tip of the right forefinger; 8, the tip of the right middle finger; 9, the tip of the right ring finger; 10, the tip of the right little finger; 11, the right wrist joint; 12, the right elbow joint; 13, the right shoulder joint; 14, the throat center; 15, the left shoulder joint; 16, the left elbow joint; 17, the left wrist joint; 18, the tip of the left thumb; 19, the tip of the left

forefinger; 20, the tip of the left middle finger; 21, the tip
of the left ring finger; 22, the tip of the left little finger;
23, the left wrist joint; 24, the left elbow joint; 25, the left
shoulder joint; 26, the throat center; 27, the heart center
between the two breasts; 28, the right breast; 29, the heart
center; 30, the left breast; 31, the heart center; 32, the
navel center; 33, the center of the abdomen; 34, the right
hip joint; 35, the right knee joint; 36, the right ankle joint;
37, the tip of the right big toe; 38, the tip of the right second toe; 39, the tip of the right middle toe; 40, the tip of
the right fourth toe; 41, the tip of the right little toe; 42,
the right ankle joint; 43, the right knee joint; 44, the right
hip joint; 45, the center of the abdomen; 46, the left hip
joint; 47, the left knee joint; 48, the left ankle joint; 49, the
tip of the left big toe; 50, the tip of the left second toe; 51,
the tip of the left middle toe; 52, the tip of the left fourth
toe; 53, the tip of the left little toe; 54, the left ankle joint;
55, the left knee joint; 56, the left hip joint; 57, the center
of the abdomen; 58, the navel center; 59, the heart center;
60, the throat center; 61, the center of the forehead. This
completes the Sixty-one Points exercise.

Shithali Karana

The second exercise is deeper than Sixty-one Points.
It is called *shithali karana*, but it can also just be called
relaxation. There is no exercise known to be higher and
better than this exercise to alleviate stress. Teachers, doctors, and therapists should understand this exercise. It is
a wonderful relaxation method. In my own experience,
forty-one insomnia cases were cured completely in seven
days with the help of this exercise. In clinical tests, the
blood sugar dropped twenty-five percent. It is also good
for hypertension. Though it can be used to prevent

insomnia, it should not be used to fall asleep. If you do it well, you do not need much sleep, but it is not an exercise used to go to sleep: it is an exercise for relaxation.

If you do this exercise, you will find a difference in the quality of your sleep. In seven days' time it completely changes the whole cycle and anatomy of sleep; the quality of sleep increases and the duration of sleep decreases. Usually you do not really get a deep sleep so that your body is fully rested; you have aches and pains and inertia in the morning. If you do this exercise you will not experience those any longer.

This exercise also is very good for either mentally based or physically based depression. If you do this exercise before meditating, you will find a difference in the quality of your meditation. Actually this should be done between pranayama and meditation.

Practice this exercise for a long time and perfect it. You should have mastery over this exercise and do it accurately. Find out where you are committing mistakes, and then correct your mistakes. You should train your body to follow your mental instructions by doing this exercise.

To begin, the room should be made dark, and the eyes should be closed. You may use something to cover your eyes. You should avoid noises from outside because they will create a disturbance in the mind. Put a pillow beneath your head, otherwise the finer gases from your digestive system can come up and disturb your heart. (Heart patients should know that gastric problems can disturb the heart, disrupt the heart rhythm, and disturb the brain.) The pillow should be neither too big nor too small, but rather a normal-sized pillow. Lie on the floor in shavasana. Let there be a space between your arms and your body, and a space between your two legs. Do not do this exercise lying on your bed or mattress. Do not allow your spinal column to be curved.

First, breathe diaphragmatically five times: five complete exhalations and five inhalations. As you exhale let your abdomen contract, allowing the lungs to expel the carbon dioxide. Let the abdominal muscles gently relax when you inhale. Exhale and inhale with diaphragmatic breathing. Now exhale from the crown of your head to the toes, and inhale from the toes to the crown of your head. There should be no jerks or noises, and the breathing should not be shallow. Exhale as though you are breathing down to the toes, relaxing. As you are exhaling you are emptying yourself and expelling all your toxins and your fatigue, stress, and strain. Inhaling, know that you are inhaling energy from the atmosphere. Inhale from your toes up through your ankles, knees, hip joints, and your spinal column, coming back to the crown of the head. Do not retain the breath. Exhale back to your toes. Do this ten times, and then exhale and inhale from your ankles, energizing your knees, hip joints, spinal column, and the crown of your head ten times. Then, exhale through the spinal column to your knees, and inhale from your knees to the crown of your head, through your spinal column, ten times. Exhale to your perineum.

At each center of concentration from the perineum upwards, exhale and inhale five times. Try to reduce the moment or pause that you create between inhalation and exhalation. See that your breath does not have any jerks or pauses in it; it should be smooth and serene. Inhale from your perineum to the crown of your head five times. Exhale to your navel center, and then inhale from there to the crown. Exhale to your heart center. Inhale from your heart center to the crown of your head. Exhale to your throat center. Inhale from your throat center to the crown of your head. Exhale to the bridge between the two nostrils and then inhale to the crown of your head. The breath should become very fine and short. At this place in the exercise, the motion of your lungs will have a shorter rhythm. Inhale from between the two nostrils to the crown of your head five times. Then let your consciousness and mind attend to the inhalation and exhalation process between the nostrils and the space between the two eyebrows. Do this at least ten times.

As a result you will find your pulse rate drop and your heart muscle able to rest. The involuntary system also rests; the pumping station that pumps blood to your brain slows down.

Again, breathe five times as though you are breathing from the crown of your head to the center of the nostrils. Next, exhale to your throat and then inhale from your throat to the crown of your head five times. Exhale to the space between the two breasts, and inhale back to the crown. Exhale from your manipura chakra and back, and then exhale to your perineum and back.

According to the scriptures, the second chakra is bypassed in this procedure. Exhale and inhale five times to your perineum and back, through the spinal column. Then exhale to the knee joints ten times, and inhale to the crown of your head. Exhale to your ankles ten times, and inhale from your ankles to the crown of your head. Exhale to your toes ten times, and inhale from the toes to the crown of your head. Then gently get up.

Throughout this entire exercise relax your whole body and let it inhale and exhale in a natural manner. When you inhale you are filling up the depth of your being with energy. When you exhale, you are cleansing your body and emptying your mind of strain, stress, and worries. Exhale and empty yourself. Inhale and fill your whole being with energy.

Agni sara

You should also know, understand, and do *agni sara*. It is a very unique and useful exercise that has the benefits of all the other exercises. If you cannot do any other physical exercise on a particular day, at least do this one exercise. It cures many diseases.

Agni sara is different from the stomach lift—it is important not to confuse the two. Unlike the stomach lift, which focuses at the navel center, agni sara is an exercise for the lower abdomen and pelvic region. It energizes the entire solar system of the body. The solar system is the largest network in the human body, and agni sara provides warmth to this entire system.

To do agni sara, stand with your feet about six inches apart and rest the weight of your body through your arms on your knees, keeping the back relaxed. Then as you exhale, contract the muscles in the lower abdomen and pull them in and up. As you inhale you gently release the muscles, allowing the lower abdomen to return to its natural position. When you pull in the abdomen it helps you to expel all the waste gases of the lungs. When you allow the abdomen to come out, it creates more space in your lungs for oxygen. You should make this exercise a habit.

To do agni sara correctly, coordinate it with your normal breathing. You exhale, pulling in and up; and you inhale and release. Exhaling, you contract the lower abdominal muscles and the area just above the pelvis, drawing them inward and upward, more tightly; and then inhaling, you release. It is not a stomach lift; it involves the lower abdomen. This is the real agni sara.

The exercise starts with the pelvis and ends at the pelvis. If you can do agni sara 100 to 150 times a day, you do not need any other exercise. You will have so much energy you will feel like you are floating. It creates perfect digestion and terrific energy. You will become more efficient in any field. Begin the practice of agni sara with twenty-five repetitions and increase to beyond a hundred.

This exercise should not be done by pregnant or menstruating women.

Yoga Nidra

Next is the practice of yoga nidra. It is a very powerful practice that will help you. There is a system and an order to this practice. Behind the system of yoga is a philosophy called Sankhya, which means "that which explains the whole." It is a numerical system: it gave birth to the science of mathematics. This is not a modern method; it is a most ancient method. It is a numerical system you can use.

There are three methods of yoga nidra that are easy for you, and that can be practiced. Another two practices are used in monasteries, and two more are used by those who have more time for practice. In your daily life you do not have that much time, so this method, which is concrete, concise, and practical, is very useful. This is called conscious sleep; you are sleeping yet you are conscious.

The finest time to practice yoga nidra is early in the morning before the sun rises, or in the evening around sunset. It should be done when it is dark and there is no strain, stimulus, distraction, or noise from outside. In the daytime it is difficult to practice it well, but if you want to practice it, then you should make your room dark. Usually yoga nidra is not done before three o'clock in the afternoon. The best time to do yoga nidra is right after meditation if you are not tired and do not fall asleep easily. This practice should not be used for sleep or for relaxation; it should only be done for yoga nidra. To learn this method you need to have a definite time set aside so that you can practice at the same time every day.

When you do this exercise, see that you are protected from noise. A little bit of sound can agitate your nervous system and injure your brain fibers, so that is why the quiet time of night is preferred. In the beginning, ear plugs can be used, but do not use rubber plugs because there is some agent in the rubber that creates irritation. Cotton balls are fine. In advanced stages, the nostrils are closed using a particular *mudra*, or gesture of the hands. But you are not prepared for this; you are prepared for the simple yoga nidra exercise.

In the beginning you should use ten minutes for this exercise. You can use an alarm to signal the end of the time. If you do use an alarm, muffle it so that it does not startle you unduly. If you are doing this exercise for more than ten minutes in the beginning, then surely you are not doing yoga nidra but are only sleeping, because the normal capacity of brainwave relaxation is only ten minutes. Your own mind will remind you of your capacity. If you are relaxing for a long time, it means that you are going to sleep. It may feel good, but it is not conscious relaxation. Conscious relaxation only relaxes the muscles. It gives you a deeper rest, yet you remain awake.

Though you can record all the things going on, do not try to do that; it will come of itself. Try to go to deep sleep. You can have a tape recorder next to you to record your snoring if you sleep, but you should ask yourself not to snore. Many of you snore while relaxing, or snore and sleep during meditation, because either you are going beyond your own capacity, you are becoming old (even though you may be young), you have lost your stamina, you have not formed a habit, or you have overeaten.

Do not do this exercise when you have overeaten or when you are fatigued. If you are a jogger, then first jog, take your bath, and wait for at least two and a half hours. If you have done any work or have indigestion, do not do this exercise. First, give enough time to your digestion. Do not do this exercise outdoors or outside your room: you may sometimes go into a deep sleep, so you need to be safely in your own private room.

The human personality is composed of habit patterns. If yoga nidra is practiced regularly like the practice of meditation, habit will lead you spontaneously to this state. Otherwise to remain fighting mentally—because you are only practicing occasionally—brings frustration. When you think that it is difficult to practice, then it really becomes difficult. But when you decide and determine to practice, your willpower and determination will lead you to achieve what you want to do.

To begin this exercise, you should lie down in shavasana. If you do it incorrectly, it may create problems for you after a few days. For example, if there is no coordination between the two halves of the body, one hip can become tense while the other hip relaxes. You are a magnetic pole and you have two sides that need to be coordinated. You must use the correct method, but you also need to have patience and work with your body.

Do not lie either on a soft bed or the floor. Have a soft pillow and use a hard bed (preferably a wooden bed) with a thin mattress. The pillow should not be either too high or too flat: a pillow that you use comfortably for sleeping will do.

Lying in shavasana, do not spread your legs either too much or keep them too close together—they should be separated comfortably. Your body and mind know what is right. Let your mind survey whether your body is placed in a comfortable position.

Next comes the question of your focal point. The ancient manuscripts say that the governor of your life has three homes. During the waking state the ajna chakra is the governor's seat. When you are conscious you use that center because the pineal and pituitary gland centers are used more then. The ajna chakra is located between the two eyebrows because it is the seat of the mind. Your mind functions most in the waking state, so this is its prominent seat.

In the dreaming state, the mind is said to be focused at the vishuddha chakra: when you dream, the governor changes his dwelling place from the ajna chakra and now resides at the throat center. During the state of deep sleep, the governor goes to the space of the heart and lives there.

Yoga nidra has something to do with these points, but you have to systematically go from one point to another. This is a process that psychologists can use in visualization and imagery.

So first you let your mind come to the eyebrow center. Using diaphragmatic breathing, take three breaths. Allow your thoughts, even your mantra, to let go. Your eyes and ears are closed; your breath is serene. Next, with the help of your breath, shift your concentration to the throat. Visualize the moon at the throat chakra. Visualization of the moon is very good; it is very soothing and helpful. Breathe freely without any conscious control, many times. Then breathe diaphragmatically. Next breathe as though the center is the space between the two breasts—the heart center, not the navel center.

When you do the exercise and you come to the heart

center, make it the focal point, and then do your breathing. You will go to sleep, but when you see that you are losing consciousness, try to break that. Do not do the exercise for more than ten minutes. Your breath will become very fine.

When you do yoga nidra, begin by exhaling and inhaling deeply. Practice the Sixty-one Points exercise, then do shithali karana. Exhale as though you are exhaling to the toes, emptying yourself of all fatigue and tension. Inhale from the toes to the crown of your head. Exhale again to your ankles and then come back, inhaling the energy from the cosmos into the region of the ankles. Inhale, filling the depth of your being with the energy that you have received. Then breathe from the crown of your head to your knees, exhaling. Inhale back to the crown of your head. Exhale to your perineum, and inhale back to the crown of your head. Exhale to your navel center, the fire of the manipura chakra, and then come back to the crown of your head. Breathe from the crown to your heart chakra, and inhale back to the crown of the head. Exhale to your throat chakra, and inhale back to the crown of your head. Exhale to the bridge of your nostrils, where you can locate both nostrils flowing freely, awakening sushumna. If one nostril is blocked, ask your mind to open it for you, and if it is your friend, your mind will do it. Now breathe between the bridge of the nostrils and the crown of the head.

In the lower limbs, breathe ten times. Do this exercise in order, exhaling and inhaling five times from muladhara to sahasrara, and for each point above muladhara. When you inhale from the nostrils to the crown of the head your breath will be become very short but it is a fine breath. It is not really shallow, but actually deep and fine, and during this time your heart muscles and involuntary nervous system will rest. Your pulse and heart rate will decrease and your brain will also rest.

When you come back to the ajna chakra, the space between the eyebrows, the inhalation and exhalation are just a feeling. Your mind is alert, watching that you are inhaling from the tip of your nostrils to the space between the eyebrows. During this time your heart rate cannot be located by a stethoscope. Your heart is completely rested. At first, because the practice is new for you, you may feel uneasy. Again, breathe as though you are breathing from the crown of your head through the nose bridge. Do this five times.

Then go back to the throat center and inhale to the crown of your head. Then exhale and inhale to the heart center and back to the crown. You continue on back to the toes. As you exhale and inhale to each point, the energy of the atmosphere or cosmos is there and is free to you.

Your mind is occupied only with inhalation and exhalation. After doing each point with the proper number of breaths, you turn onto your left side and continue to breathe so that if there is any undigested food in the system it can be digested—undigested food creates digestive and gastric problems that are uncomfortable.

Breathe from head to toe and toe to head—but breathe freely with the whole body, without touching on those points: exhale and inhale as though your whole right side is exhaling and inhaling ten times. Then turn onto the right side.

Do the same thing on the right side. Exhale and inhale ten times as if the left side breathes. Then again shift onto your back. Let your whole body inhale and exhale. Exhale as though your whole body is exhaling. Let your limbs feel as if they were receiving energy through the nose and pores. Feel as if your whole body is being energized, and anything that is injurious to your body is being thrown out and expelled.

Now, practice yoga nidra. Shift your attention from the eyebrow center, to the throat center, and finally to the heart center; and be centered there. Do not think about your posture or anything else. Just be aware at the space between the two breasts. When you end the exercise, bring your attention systematically outward.

CHAPTER TWELVE

Conclusion

*S*O WE HAVE DISCUSSED the stages of an inward journey—the journey from the gross to the subtle, and from the mere self to the highest self. If you systematically follow the steps of the internal journey, it will help you. Your goal on this journey is to learn the practices and to awaken the reservoir of fire that is already within you. If you do this you can be free of the endless cycle of the world, with its snares and bondage, and then you can lead the mind to a state beyond. This awakening is the goal of the path of fire and light—the light of knowledge, truth, understanding, and love. You can completely transform yourself and attain the highest state in this life.

What I have written here I have written on the basis of my own experience and the encounters I had with many sages. Disappointingly, I find these days that aspirants do not seem to aspire to lead a balanced life. They search for perfection in the external world, ignoring human potentials and internal states. There is no coherence or harmony, and thus in our society today the leaders and the intelligentsia seem drawn to building hospitals and research centers to cure diseases that actually are born because of our ignorance, sloth, and lack of awareness. When you become aware that human resources in the interior self are immense, and try to probe into the subtler realms within, you will come across unbelievable phenomena. These are actually not alien but are your own potential, buried deeply in the unconscious.

The program we have outlined will guide you systematically on this path—but you must practice! You cannot attain any grace or assistance from outside until you have learned to cultivate your own grace, through working systematically with your mind and determination. When you cultivate the ascending power, then the descending power of grace also dawns. The library of knowledge and capacities within yourself can definitely be brought forward, but you must first cultivate your own strength.

To do that, remember that you need to accomplish eight major points. First, you need to develop the habit of a regular, systematic meditation time and practice. Secondly, you need to learn to conduct an internal dialogue with yourself, so that the mind is prepared for meditation. Third, your posture must be made still, steady, and erect, so that your body does not distort your breathing or distract your mind. Fourth, you need to make the breath serene and calm, gradually quieting body and mind. Fifth, you need to cultivate sankalpa, your own determination that "I can do it, I will do it, I must do it." Sixth, you will have to learn how to let go of disturbing or interfering thoughts and learn not to invite such distractions. Seventh, you should cultivate the quality of introspection—that is, inspecting within: inspecting the thoughts that arise and determining which thought patterns assist your meditation, and which are obstacles. Eighth, you then need to learn to witness your thoughts and observe them without reaction.

This is a complete and comprehensive program for following the path of the inner journey, and nothing you learn in the external world will help you as much as this internal process. The peace and solace you seek in the external world is already within you—but you need to experience this! That Light within you is a ripple of the ocean of bliss, a ripple of the Infinite or Absolute. This is your essential nature and this is what you have come here to know. You should learn to have confidence in this Light of Life, confidence in yourself, and confidence in your spiritual tradition.

Now, is it possible for a modern person to practice or devote so much time to understanding the mystery of death: life here and hereafter? It is not at all difficult, provided one decides to fearlessly examine and explore the finer dimensions of life and not remain lingering, unsatisfied, living with the transitory objectives of the world, thinking and believing that the external world alone exists and offers happiness to the human mind and soul. Some modern writers consider such subjects to be occult. Such writers are not educated thoroughly enough to talk, discuss, and write on these subjects. If everything is considered to be difficult, then what is easy? "Difficult" and "impossible" are concepts or limitations of the human mind. While you have an immense capacity to explore the many dimensions and totality of your mind, you do not have to retreat from the world and go into seclusion. Rather, devote some time to practicing meditation, without any qualifications or limitations—such as Christian meditation, Jain meditation, Hindu meditation, or Sufi meditation. Meditation is meditation. It is a journey that leads you from the gross level of awareness to the subtlest level of awareness. On the way, students find themselves coming across many potentials of which they are ordinarily unaware.

To know yourself, you do not have to renounce—but you must learn to adjust so that you can be content here in this lifetime. It is true that "like attracts like," and as you are on the path, you are guided by an inner sense to meet fellow travelers who share their experiences with you. Spirituality is not the property of any culture, religion, sect, color, or sex: anyone who aspires, desires, determines, and practices will attain it.

As we grow from childhood onwards, in the end there is a point that is called death. Death is a point of growth. Though a parting day, death actually is a wedding day, when separation is not really separation but rather leads you to a fresh, glorious hope that is called life hereafter. The wise do not mourn, remain afraid, or worry, for death is an essential part of growth; it is a must. Aspirants should remember that a day is bound to come when they will have to part from this world, and they should be prepared. There are two parts of sadhana: preparing yourself to practice, and then practicing sincerely and regularly, by watching your mental habits, patterns, and behavior. The law of karma says if you perform an action you are bound to receive the fruits. Therefore, you should not feel or think that you are incapable of practicing the science of yoga.

Now, at present, you have no control or understanding over your unconscious life, that unknown part that constantly motivates you. The wonderful method of yoga nidra will help you in going within. You are trying to reach and touch the infinite Source, which is only One, self-existent. You have the capacity to do that. No human being is weak. You make yourself weak when you become the victim of your habit patterns, your senses, and when your mind starts identifying itself with the objects of the world. Yet if you also learn to observe your actions you can learn about your unconscious mind and remove that aspect of mind that stands as a barrier between you and Reality.

You have two selves: a mere self and a higher self. That mere self has been playing the part of the higher self—and the higher self has become the mere self. That is the cause of your agony. The mere self is limited by the boundaries of your senses; the higher self is not within the realm of your senses. The mere self means the body, senses, breath, conscious mind, and unconscious mind. This is the mere self because it does not exist itself independently; it is not self-existent.

According to Vedantic literature there are three definitions of truth: first, that which is self-existent and does not need any other object to lean upon; second, that which is eternal, is never born and never dies; and third, that which encompasses the whole universe, which includes all and excludes none, which is *purna*, or "complete in itself." Truth is that which has the power to be in the smallest particle—and in the largest tissue of the universe. Truth is self-existent; it was never born, so it never dies; it includes all and excludes none. This is the definition of absolute truth.

How can that absolute truth be realized in your daily life? To realize it means being aware of truth as you function in the external world—as you work, talk to people, do your duties, and discipline your children and students.

Meditation in action is awareness of truth all the time. When you have learned to do meditation in silence, then the next step is to keep that meditation fresh and green, to keep that flame alive—and to do that you have to learn meditation in action. There is a clear procedure for this, and it requires that you understand your mind and the states of consciousness.

Don't become dependent on any external resource on this path, but learn to deal constructively with the external world. To do that, learn to make every external circumstance into a means for your progress, not an obstacle. If you learn to make all your relationships in the external world into means, you will definitely make progress. The process of learning to serve and give to others selflessly will help you to come out of that mire of selfishness and negativity that results when you merely strengthen your ego, constantly seeking to develop only "I, me, and mine." External love and service is one very important step toward freedom. You cannot become enlightened by evading or escaping the world: the world exists to help you progress, and all the things of the world exist for you to use as means.

If you do your practice it is not possible that you will fail to make progress, although you often do not see the subtle process and progress at deeper levels. The gurus impart the best of their knowledge, the heart of their teaching, in silence. And when you are in silence within, they communicate with you at that level. Do your practice if you want to make progress.

Above all else, remember this one thing: it is easy to meet that Infinity within—to attain this awareness, you just have to be silent and quiet. When you calm your mind and make it one-pointed, it can penetrate those fields of the mind that are not ordinarily penetrated by humans, and then you will perceive the Reality within.

This awakening is called fire, and the knowledge through which you are doing all this is called light—the light of knowledge, the light of discrimination, the light of understanding, the light of love and knowledge. You need both fire and light—and they are one and the same.

Glossary

Agni sara. A yogic kriya or exercise that involves lifting the abdominal muscles and pulling up the pelvis gradually to strengthen the navel center. It is also known as the abdominal lift.

Ahimsa. Non-injury, non-hurting, non-killing. It is one of the highest of all observances leading to spiritual goals.

Ajna chakra. The sixth chakra, situated between the eyebrows; the seat of the mind.

Aklishta. "Not painful, not afflicted, pure." This term is used in *Yoga Sutras 1.5*, and connotes thoughts that do not lead to worldly attachment and that contribute toward self-realization.

Amara. Not subject to death and decay. Used in reference to those great souls who are beyond birth and death and who may appear on this plane to help humanity.

Anahata chakra. The heart center, the center of the air element; an important chakra for the practice of meditation.

Anahata nada. "Unstruck sound." In the silence found at the heart center a sound arises which is not caused by any physical means. This sound is known only in deep meditation.

Antahkarana. The inner instrument. The intellect, ego, sensory-motor mind, and storehouse of memories can be considered to be the inner instruments of cognition.

Aparavidya. Knowledge of "this" plane; of the apparent, phenomenal reality. Literally, "not-beyond-knowledge." Compare *paravidya*.

Apta mahapurusha. A trustworthy person, a great person, one who speaks in accord with the way he thinks and acts; one whose speech and actions convey truth.

Atman. The pure self. According to Indian philosophy the self is eternal, and its essential nature is existence, consciousness, and bliss. It permeates the waking, dreaming, and deep sleep states and remains above all mundane pains and pleasures.

Avadhuta. A supremely self-realized soul who functions through a mind and body, but whose consciousness extends to the Infinite.

Avatar. A divine incarnation. After death, realized beings can choose to incarnate onto the physical plane in order to serve humanity. Ordinary mortals are merely reborn to continue their growth process and do not have the choice of remaining beyond.

Bandha. A lock, or control. There are many kinds of locks applied during the practice of pranayama; among them the root, navel, and chin locks are most important. Locks are used to hold and channel energy.

Bhoga. Sensual experience or enjoyment. The material world as the object of experience; the pleasant or painful experience one has during his life as the result of karma.

Bhogi. One who pursues sensual pleasure.

Bhukti. Enjoyment of the things of the world.

Bhuta. An element. In Indian philosophy the universe is thought to be composed of five elemental substances: earth, water, fire, air, and ether.

Bija mantra. Seed mantra. In the science of mantra certain letters or phonemes are supposed to be the foci of divine powers or vibratory patterns of certain elements.

Bindu. A dot or point. A point associated with the chakras may be assigned to students by their teacher for concentration.

Buddhi. The intellect, the decisive faculty.

Chakra. Wheel or circle. In the yogic tradition it refers to a center of consciousness. There are said to be seven or more of these located within the human being, ranging from the base of the spine to the top of the head.

Deva. Bright being or celestial being. Devas are said to be superior to other beings because of the predominance of sattva in them.

Guru. The popular term used for a spiritual master who reveals the path of divinity to his students. It is a term indicating great reverence and humility. Traditionally the term "guru" is not used by itself without "deva." *Gurudeva* literally means "the bright being who dispels the darkness of ignorance."

Gurubhai. "Guru-brother." A fellow student in yoga, studying with the same master.

Ida. One of the three nadis, corresponding to lunar energy and situated on the left side of the spinal column.

Janman. Birth. Birth simply means coming to an external state of existence. The soul is exactly the same before and after birth; it is "behind and comes forward."

Jiva. The individuated soul that identifies itself with the body-mind organism.

Kaula. One of the three tantric paths.

Klishta. "Afflicted, painful, impure." As used in *Yoga Sutras 1.5*, it connotes thoughts that are stained by their attachment to worldly experience and that lead to attachment and continued bondage.

Kriya. A wash or method of purification.

Kumbhaka. Suspension of breath; breath retention.

Kunda. The pit or bowl. The center where kundalini sleeps, or abides in her latent form.

Kundalini. Creative energy in a static state, the spiritual force itself, the "Grand Potential." The dormant energy of shakti.

Manipura chakra. "Filled with jewels." The third chakra, the center of fire, the navel center.

Mishra. One of the three tantric paths.

Moksha. The liberation which is attained upon realizing the true nature of the self. This is the state in which one is no longer subject to worldly influences.

Mukta. A liberated one; one who is not in the bondage of pain, because he realizes his essential nature.

Mukti. Liberation.

Mulabandha. The root lock, performed by contracting the anal muscle upward.

Muladhara chakra. The root support chakra situated at the base of the spine, the center of the earth element.

Nada. The celestial sound that yogis hear internally. By contemplating on this sound, the mind becomes focused and inward.

Nadi.   Energy channel. According to yoga manuals, there are 72,000 nadis, among which fourteen are most important.

Para-atman.   The transcendental self; Reality.

Para-kaya pravesha.   The science of consciously dropping a body and getting into another body.

Paravidya.   Knowledge of the beyond. The knowledge of the Supreme, which cannot be achieved through books and other methods of conventional study and education. Compare *aparavidya*.

Paramshiva.   Transcendent consciousness.

Pingala.   One of the three major energy channels, situated along the right side of the spinal column, corresponding to the solar energy in the body.

Prakriti.   Primordial nature. According to the Sankhya and Yoga systems of philosophy, there are two eternal realities: purusha and prakriti. Prakriti is the unconscious principle and the cause of all worldly phenomena.

Prana.   The life-force. In yogic tradition the life-force or prana is said to be tenfold, depending on its nature and function.

Pranayama.   Breathing exercises used to control the movement of prana.

Puraka.   Inhalation.

Purna.   Fullness, perfection, completion.

Purusha.   The conscious principle; the pure self. Through association with purusha, prakriti becomes the enjoyer of pain, pleasure, and indifference.

Rajas.   The force of activity and movement. One of the attributes of prakriti.

Rechaka.   Exhalation.

Sadhaka.   One who follows the spiritual path.

Sahasrara chakra.   The center of consciousness located at the crown of the head, the thousand-petaled lotus.

Samadhi.   Spiritual absorption; the eighth rung of raja yoga.

Samaya.   One of the three tantric paths.

Samskara.   A subtle impression of a past action.

Sankalpa shakti.   The power of determination. In spiritual practice, this power is the foundation of progress.

Satsanga.   Company of the sages.

Sattva.   One of the attributes of prakriti. The quality of light and illumination.

Satya.   Truth. Satya is also the second yogic virtue, the practice of truthfulness.

Shakti.   The power. The dynamic aspect of Consciousness, the source of the manifest world and its activities.

Shava.   A corpse.

Shavasana.   The corpse pose, a posture for relaxation.

Shiva.   Pure consciousness, existence, and bliss. In contrast to Shakti, Shiva is the static state of consciousness.

Shithali karana.   An advanced exercise for relaxation, and a preparation for yoga nidra.

Siddhasana.   The accomplished pose, which is required exclusively in the practice of some of the advanced pranayamas.

Siddhi.   A power or accomplishment that is achieved through various yogic practices such as pranayama or mantra japa and that accompanies inner development.

So-ham.   The mantra associated with breathing. "So" is the sound of inhalation, and "ham" is the sound of exhalation. These words mean "I am that."

Srishti.   That which is hidden and comes forward (is born).

Sukhamana.   A joyful or pleasant mind, associated with the sushumna nadi.

Sukhasana.   The easy pose. Sitting cross-legged with head, neck, and trunk straight.

Sushumna.   The brahma nadi, also known as shakti nadi, the central channel through which kundalini travels and unites herself with Shiva in sahasrara. When the breath flows freely and equally through both nostrils, sushumna is engaged.

Sutra.   "Thread." An aphorism or unifying thread of thought.

Svadhishthana chakra.   "Her own abode." The second chakra.

Svarodaya.   The science which describes the subtleties of prana and the methods for expanding and controlling it.

Tamas.   The quality of inertia, heaviness, and darkness.

Tantra. A branch of yoga which incorporates divergent disciplines such as hatha, kundalini, external rituals, meditation, and yantra.

Tapas. Ascetic observance, power or practice, austerity, reducing one's material and physical pleasures, luxuries, and the body's dependence on objects.

Trataka. Gazing at an external object; a practice designed to enhance one-pointedness.

Turiya. The fourth, transcendental, state of consciousness, the state beyond waking, dreaming, and sleep.

Utpatti. The proces of coming forward from the unknown and unseen (being born).

Vairagya. Dispassion or nonattachment—not only withdrawal from the external world, but simultaneously uniting oneself with the higher truth.

Vidya. Knowledge, proficiency in the sacred texts, in the tradition, and particularly in the systematic method of practice.

Vishuddha chakra. The throat center, the fifth chakra. The center of space.

Yajna. Ritualistic ceremony, which can be external or internal.

Yoga nidra. Yogic sleep; a unique state of consciousness.

Index

About the Author

BORN IN 1925 in northern India, Swami Rama was raised from early childhood by a great Bengali yogi and saint who lived in the foothills of the Himalayas. In his youth he practiced the various disciplines of yoga science and philosophy in the traditional monasteries of the Himalayas and studied with many spiritual adepts, including Mahatma Gandhi, Sri Aurobindo, and Rabindranath Tagore. He also traveled to Tibet to study with his grandmaster.

He received his higher education at Bangalore, Prayaga, Varanasi, and Oxford University, England. At the age of twenty-four he became Shankaracharya of Karvirpitham in South India, the highest spiritual position in India. During this term he had a tremendous impact on the spiritual customs of that time: he dispensed with useless formalities and rituals, made it possible for all segments of society to worship in the temples, and encouraged the instruction of women in meditation. He renounced the dignity and prestige of this high office in 1952 to return to the Himalayas to intensify his yogic practices.

After completing an intense meditative practice in the cave monasteries, he emerged with the determination to serve humanity, particularly to bring the teachings of the East to the West. With the encouragement of his master, Swami Rama began his task by studying Western philosophy and psychology. He worked as a medical consultant in London and assisted in parapsychological research in Moscow. He then returned to India, where he established an ashram in Rishikesh. He completed his degree in homeopathy at the medical college in Darbhanga in 1960. He came to the United States in 1969, bringing his knowledge and wisdom to the West. His teachings combine Eastern spirituality with modern Western therapies.

Swami Rama was a freethinker, guided by his direct experience and inner wisdom, and he encouraged his students to be guided in the same way. He often told them, "I am a messenger, delivering the wisdom of the Himalayan sages of my tradition. My job is to introduce you to the teacher within."

Swami Rama came to America upon the invitation of Dr. Elmer Green of the Menninger Foundation of Topeka, Kansas, as a consultant in a research project investigating the voluntary control of involuntary states. He participated in experiments that helped to revolutionize scientific thinking about the relationship between body and mind, amazing scientists by his demonstrating, under laboratory conditions, precise conscious control of autonomic physical responses and mental functioning, feats previously thought to be impossible.

Swami Rama founded the Himalayan International Institute of Yoga Science and Philosophy, the Himalayan Institute Hospital Trust in India, and many centers throughout the world. He is the author of numerous books on health, meditation, and the yogic scriptures. Swami Rama left his body in November 1996.

The main building of the Institute headquarters, near Honesdale, Pa.

The Himalayan Institute

FOUNDED IN 1971 by Swami Rama, the Himalayan Institute has been dedicated to helping people grow physically, mentally, and spiritually by combining the best knowledge of both the East and the West.

Our international headquarters is located on a beautiful 400-acre campus in the rolling hills of the Pocono Mountains of northeastern Pennsylvania. The atmosphere here is one to foster growth, increased inner awareness, and calm. Our grounds provide a wonderfully peaceful and healthy setting for our seminars and extended programs. Students from around the world join us here to attend programs in such diverse areas as hatha yoga, meditation, stress reduction, Ayurveda, nutrition, Eastern philosophy, psychology, and other subjects. Whether the programs are for weekend meditation retreats, week-long seminars on spirituality, months-long residential programs, or holistic health services, the attempt here is to provide an environment of gentle inner progress. We invite you to join with us in the ongoing process of personal growth and development.

The Institute is a nonprofit organization. Your membership in the Institute helps to support its programs. Please call or write for information on becoming a member.

Institute Programs, Services, and Facilities

Institute programs share an emphasis on conscious holistic living and personal self-development, including:

Special weekend or extended seminars to teach skills and techniques for increasing your ability to be healthy and enjoy life

Meditation retreats and advanced meditation and philosophical instruction

Vegetarian cooking and nutritional training

Hatha yoga and exercise workshops

Residential programs for self-development

Holistic health services and Ayurvedic Rejuvenation Programs through the Institute's Center for Health and Healing.

A *Quarterly Guide to Programs and Other Offerings* is free within the USA. To request a copy, or for further information, call 800-822-4547 or 570-253-5551, fax 570-253-9078, email bqinfo@himalayaninstitute.org, write the Himalayan Institute, RR 1 Box 400, Honesdale, PA 18431-9706 USA, or visit our Web site at www.himalayaninstitute.org.

The Himalayan Institute Press

THE HIMALAYAN INSTITUTE PRESS has long been regarded as "The Resource for Holistic Living." We publish dozens of titles, as well as audio and video tapes, that offer practical methods for living harmoniously and achieving inner balance. Our approach addresses the whole person—body, mind, and spirit—integrating the latest scientific knowledge with ancient healing and self-development techniques.

As such, we offer a wide array of titles on physical and psychological health and well-being, spiritual growth through meditation and other yogic practices, as well as translations of yogic scriptures.

Our sidelines include the Japa Kit for meditation practice, the original Neti™ Pot, the ideal tool for sinus and allergy sufferers, and The Breath Pillow,™ a unique tool for learning health-supportive diaphragmatic breathing.

Subscriptions are available to a bimonthly magazine, *Yoga International*, which offers thought-provoking articles on all aspects of meditation and yoga, including yoga's sister science, Ayurveda.

For a free catalog call 800-822-4547 or 570-253-5551, email hibooks@himalayaninstitute.org, fax 570-251-7812, write the Himalayan Institute Press, RR 1, Box 405, Honesdale, PA 18431-9709, USA, or visit our Web site at www.himalayaninstitute.org.